Contents

Appendices

Preface

Upon instructions by the Maritime Safety Committee (MSC), the Sub-Committee on Containers and Cargoes (which was later superseded by the Sub-Committee on Dangerous Goods, Solid Cargoes and Containers) developed the Code of Safe Practice for Cargo Stowage and Securing. The Code was approved by the Committee at its fifty-eighth session (May 1990) and was adopted by the Assembly at its seventeenth regular session (November 1991) by resolution A.714(17).

The Assembly recommended that Governments implement the Code at the earliest possible opportunity and requested the MSC to keep it under review and amend it as necessary.

The Code has undergone subsequent changes through the years. The first major change was the amendments of MSC/Circ.664, adopted at the sixty-fourth session of MSC (5 to 9 December 1994), and MSC/Circ.691, adopted by the Committee at its sixty-fifth session (9 to 17 May 1995), both of which were issued as the 1994/1995 Amendments to the Code of Safe Practice for Cargo Stowage and Securing, introducing annex 13, which was incorporated into the previous edition.

This edition includes amendments to annex 12 on safe stowage and securing of unit loads, issued as MSC/Circ.740 on 14 June 1996 at the sixty-sixth session of the Maritime Safety Committee. It also contains amendments adopted by the Committee at its seventy-fifth session (15 to 24 May 2002), issued as MSC/Circ.1026, which saw significant changes in the contents of annex 13.

The Committee, at its eighty-seventh session (12 to 21 May 2010), approved the following amendments to the Code: by MSC.1/Circ.1352 incorporating a new annex 14 – Guidance on Providing Safe Working Conditions for Securing of Containers on Deck which apply in their entirety for containerships, the keels of which were laid or which are at a similar stage of construction on or after 1 January 2015; sections 4.4 (Training and familiarization), 7.1 (Introduction), 7.3 (Maintenance) and section 8 (Specialized container safety design) apply to existing containerships, the keels of which were laid or which are at a similar stage of construction before 1 January 2015; and the principles of this guidance contained in sections 6 (Design) and 7.2 (Operational procedures) are applied to existing containerships as far as practical by the flag State Administration with the understanding that existing ships would not be required to be enlarged or undergo other major structural modifications as determined.

The Committee also approved by MSC.1/Circ.1353 – Revised guidelines for the preparation of the Cargo Securing Manual which apply in their entirety for containerships, the keels of which were laid or which are at a similar stage of construction on or after 1 January 2015 and chapters 1 to 4 apply to existing containerships, the keels of which were laid or which were at a similar stage of construction before 1 January 2015. In addition, the Committee approved by MSC.1/Circ.1354 – Amendments to the elements to be taken into account when considering the safe stowage and securing of cargo units and vehicles in ships (resolution A.533(13)); and further approved, by MSC.1/Circ.1355 – Amendments to the guidelines for securing arrangements for the transport of road vehicles on ro–ro ships (resolution A.581(14)), as amended by MSC/Circ.812.

Resolution A.714(17)
adopted on 6 November 1991, as amended

Code of Safe Practice for Cargo Stowage and Securing

THE ASSEMBLY,

RECALLING Article 15(j) of the Convention on the International Maritime Organization concerning the functions of the Assembly in relation to regulations and guidelines concerning maritime safety,

RECALLING ALSO resolution A.489(XII) on safe stowage and securing of cargo units and other entities in ships other than cellular containerships and MSC/Circ.385[*] of January 1985 containing the provisions to be included in a cargo securing manual to be carried on board ships,

RECALLING FURTHER resolution A.533(13) on elements to be taken into account when considering the safe stowage and securing of cargo units and vehicles in ships,

CONSIDERING the revised IMO/ILO Guidelines for packing cargo in freight containers or vehicles,[†]

CONSIDERING ALSO resolution A.581(14) on guidelines for securing arrangements for the transport of road vehicles on ro–ro ships,

BEARING IN MIND that a number of serious accidents have occurred as a result of inadequate securing arrangements on board and deficient stowage and securing of cargoes in vehicles and containers, and that only proper stowage and securing of cargo on adequately designed and properly equipped ships can prevent the occurrence of such accidents in the future,

---

[*] MSC/Circ.385 was revoked by MSC/Circ.745 of 13 June 1996, which was superseded by MSC.1/Circ.1353.

[†] These Guidelines have been replaced by the IMO/ILO/UN ECE Guidelines for packing of cargo transport units.

RECOGNIZING the need to improve the stowage and securing of cargoes shown by experience to create specific hazards to the safety of ships, and the stowage and securing of road vehicles transported on board ro–ro ships,

RECOGNIZING FURTHER that such improvement could be achieved by the establishment of a composite code of safe practice for cargo stowage and securing on board ships, including packing or loading cargo in road vehicles and freight containers,

BELIEVING that the application of such a code of safe practice would enhance maritime safety,

HAVING CONSIDERED the recommendations made by the Maritime Safety Committee at its fifty-eighth session,

1.   ADOPTS the Code of Safe Practice for Cargo Stowage and Securing set out in the annex to the present resolution;

2.   URGES Governments to implement this Code at the earliest possible opportunity;

3.   REQUESTS the Maritime Safety Committee to keep this Code under review and to amend it, as necessary;

4.   REVOKES resolution A.288(VIII).

Code of Safe Practice for Cargo Stowage and Securing

Foreword

The proper stowage and securing of cargoes is of the utmost importance for the safety of life at sea. Improper stowage and securing of cargoes has resulted in numerous serious ship casualties and caused injury and loss of life, not only at sea but also during loading and discharge.

In order to deal with the problems and hazards arising from improper stowage and securing of certain cargoes on ships, the International Maritime Organization (IMO) has issued guidelines in the form of either Assembly resolutions or circulars adopted by the Maritime Safety Committee (MSC); these are listed hereunder:

- Safe stowage and securing of cargo units and other entities in ships other than cellular containerships, resolution A.489(XII) [see appendix 1];

- Revised guidelines for the preparation of the Cargo Securing Manual, MSC.1/Circ.1353 [see appendix 2];

- Elements to be taken into account when considering the safe stowage and securing of cargo units and vehicles in ships, resolution A.533(13), as amended [see appendix 3];

- Guidelines for securing arrangements for the transport of road vehicles on ro–ro ships, resolution A.581(14), as amended [see appendix 4];

- IMO/ILO/UN ECE Guidelines for packing of cargo transport units [see the Supplement to the IMDG Code (sales number IH210E)];

- Recommendations for entering enclosed spaces aboard ships, resolution A.864(20) [see appendix 5].

The accelerations acting on a ship in a seaway result from a combination of longitudinal, vertical and predominantly transverse motions. The forces created by these accelerations give rise to the majority of securing problems.

The hazards arising from these forces should be dealt with by taking measures both to ensure proper stowage and securing of cargoes on board and to reduce the amplitude and frequency of ship motions.

The purpose of this Code is to provide an international standard to promote the safe stowage and securing of cargoes by:

- drawing the attention of shipowners and ship operators to the need to ensure that the ship is suitable for its intended purpose;

- providing advice to ensure that the ship is equipped with proper cargo securing means;

- providing general advice concerning the proper stowage and securing of cargoes to minimize the risks to the ship and personnel;

- providing specific advice on those cargoes which are known to create difficulties and hazards with regard to their stowage and securing;

- advising on actions which may be taken in heavy sea conditions; and

- advising on actions which may be taken to remedy the effects of cargo shifting.

In providing such advice, it should be borne in mind that the master is responsible for the safe conduct of the voyage and the safety of the ship, its crew and its cargo.

General principles

All cargoes should be stowed and secured in such a way that the ship and persons on board are not put at risk.

The safe stowage and securing of cargoes depend on proper planning, execution and supervision.

Personnel commissioned to tasks of cargo stowage and securing should be properly qualified and experienced.

Personnel planning and supervising the stowage and securing of cargo should have a sound practical knowledge of the application and content of the Cargo Securing Manual, if provided.

In all cases, improper stowage and securing of cargo will be potentially hazardous to the securing of other cargoes and to the ship itself.

Decisions taken for measures of stowage and securing cargo should be based on the most severe weather conditions which may be expected by experience for the intended voyage.

Ship-handling decisions taken by the master, especially in bad weather conditions, should take into account the type and stowage position of the cargo and the securing arrangements.

Chapter 1
General

1.1 Application

This Code applies to cargoes carried on board ships (other than solid and liquid bulk cargoes and timber stowed on deck) and, in particular, to those cargoes whose stowage and securing have proved in practice to create difficulties.

1.2 Definitions of the terms used

For the purposes of this Code:

Cargo unit means a vehicle, container, flat, pallet, portable tank, packaged unit, or any other entity, etc., and loading equipment, or any part thereof, which belongs to the ship but is not fixed to the ship as defined in Assembly resolution A.489(XII).

Intermediate bulk container (IBC) means a rigid, semi-rigid or flexible portable bulk container packaging of a capacity of not more than 3 m^3 (3,000 ℓ), designed for mechanical handling and tested for its satisfactory resistance to handling and transport stresses.

Portable tank means a tank which is not permanently secured on board a ship, and has a capacity of more than 450 ℓ and a shell fitted with external stabilizing members and items of service equipment and structural equipment necessary for the transport of gases, liquids or solids.

Road tank-vehicle means a vehicle with wheels and fitted with a tank or tanks intended for the transport of gases, liquids or solids by both road and sea modes of transport, the tank or tanks of which are rigidly and permanently attached to the vehicle during all normal operations of loading, transport and discharge and are neither filled nor emptied on board.

Road vehicle means a commercial vehicle, semi-trailer, road train, articulated road train or a combination of vehicles, as defined in Assembly resolution A.581(14), as amended.

Roll-trailer means a low vehicle for the carriage of cargo with one or more wheel axles on the rear and a support on the front end, which is towed or pushed in the port to and from its stowage on board the ship by a special tow-vehicle.

Ro–ro ship means a ship which has one or more decks either closed or open, not normally subdivided in any way and generally running the entire length of the ship, carrying goods which are loaded and unloaded normally in a horizontal manner.

Unit load means that a number of packages are either:

.1   placed or stacked, and secured by strapping, shrink-wrapping or other suitable means, on to a load board such as a pallet; or

.2   placed in a protective outer packaging such as a pallet box; or

.3   permanently secured together in a sling.

1.3   Forces

1.3.1   Forces which have to be absorbed by suitable arrangements for stowage and securing to prevent cargo shifting are generally composed of components acting relative to the axes of the ship:

- longitudinal;

- transverse; and

- vertical.

Remark: For the purpose of stowage and securing cargo, longitudinal and transverse forces are considered predominant.

1.3.2   Transverse forces alone, or the resultant of transverse, longitudinal and vertical forces, normally increase with the height of the stow and the longitudinal distance of the stow from the ship's centre of motion in a seaway. The most severe forces can be expected in the furthest forward, the furthest aft and the highest stowage position on each side of the ship.

1.3.3   The transverse forces exerted increase directly with the metacentric height of the ship. An undue metacentric height may be caused by:

- improper design of the ship;

- unsuitable cargo distribution; and

- unsuitable bunker and ballast distribution.

1.3.4   Cargo should be so distributed that the ship has a metacentric height in excess of the required minimum and, whenever practicable, within an acceptable upper limit to minimize the forces acting on the cargo.

1.3.5   In addition to the forces referred to above, cargo carried on deck may be subjected to forces arising from the effects of wind and green seas.

1.3.6   Improper shiphandling (course or speed) may create adverse forces acting on the ship and the cargo.

1.3.7   The magnitude of the forces may be estimated by using the appropriate calculation methods as contained in the Cargo Securing Manual, if provided.

1.3.8   Although the operation of anti-roll devices may improve the behaviour of the ship in a seaway, the effect of such devices should not be taken into account when planning the stowage and securing of cargoes.

1.4   Behaviour of cargoes

1.4.1   Some cargoes have a tendency to deform or to compact themselves during the voyage, which will result in a slackening of their securing gear.

1.4.2   Cargoes with low friction coefficients, when stowed without proper friction-increasing devices such as dunnage, soft boards, rubber mats, etc., are difficult to secure unless tightly stowed across the ship.

1.5   Criteria for estimating the risk of cargo shifting

1.5.1   When estimating the risk of cargo shifting, the following should be considered:

- dimensional and physical properties of the cargo;
- location of the cargo and its stowage on board;
- suitability of the ship for the particular cargo;
- suitability of the securing arrangements for the particular cargo;
- expected seasonal weather and sea conditions;
- expected ship behaviour during the intended voyage;
- stability of the ship;
- geographical area of the voyage; and
- duration of the voyage.

1.5.2 These criteria should be taken into account when selecting suitable stowage and securing methods and whenever reviewing the forces to be absorbed by the securing equipment.

1.5.3 Bearing in mind the above criteria, the master should accept the cargo on board his ship only if he is satisfied that it can be safely transported.

1.6   Cargo Securing Manual

1.6.1 Ships carrying cargo units and other entities covered in this Code and as outlined in resolution A.489(XII) (appendix 1) should carry a Cargo Securing Manual as detailed in MSC.1/Circ.1353.[*]

1.6.2 The cargo securing arrangements detailed in the ship's Cargo Securing Manual, if provided, should be based on the forces expected to affect the cargo carried by the ship, calculated in accordance with the method described in annex 13 or with a method accepted by the Administration or approved by a classification society acceptable to the Administration.

1.7   Equipment

The ship's cargo securing equipment should be:

- available in sufficient quantity;
- suitable for its intended purpose, taking into account the recommendations of the Cargo Securing Manual, if provided;
- of adequate strength;
- easy to use; and
- well maintained.

1.8   Special cargo transport units

The shipowner and the ship operator should, where necessary, make use of relevant expertise when considering the shipment of a cargo with unusual characteristics which may require special attention to be given to its location on board vis-à-vis the structural strength of the ship, its stowage and securing, and the weather conditions which may be expected during the intended voyage.

---

[*] See appendix 2.

1.9   Cargo information

1.9.1   Prior to shipment the shipper should provide all necessary information about the cargo to enable the shipowner or ship operator to ensure that:

- the different commodities to be carried are compatible with each other or suitably separated;

- the cargo is suitable for the ship;

- the ship is suitable for the cargo; and

- the cargo can be safely stowed and secured on board the ship and transported under all expected conditions during the intended voyage.

1.9.2   The master should be provided with adequate information regarding the cargo to be carried so that its stowage may be properly planned for handling and transport.

Chapter 2
Principles of safe stowage and securing of cargoes

2.1   Suitability of cargo for transport

Cargo carried in containers, road vehicles, shipborne barges, railway wagons and other cargo transport units should be packed and secured within these units so as to prevent, throughout the voyage, damage or hazard to the ship, to the persons on board and to the marine environment.

2.2   Cargo distribution

2.2.1   It is of utmost importance that the master takes great care in planning and supervising the stowage and securing of cargoes in order to prevent cargo sliding, tipping, racking, collapsing, etc.

2.2.2   The cargo should be distributed so as to ensure that the stability of the ship throughout the entire voyage remains within acceptable limits so that the hazards of excessive accelerations are reduced as far as practicable.

2.2.3   Cargo distribution should be such that the structural strength of the ship is not adversely affected.

2.3   Cargo securing arrangements

2.3.1   Particular care should be taken to distribute forces as evenly as practicable between the cargo securing devices. If this is not feasible, the arrangements should be upgraded accordingly.

2.3.2   If, due to the complex structure of a securing arrangement or other circumstances, the person in charge is unable to assess the suitability of the arrangement from experience and knowledge of good seamanship, the arrangement should be verified by using an acceptable calculation method.

2.4   Residual strength after wear and tear

Cargo securing arrangements and equipment should have sufficient residual strength to allow for normal wear and tear during their lifetime.

2.5   Friction forces

Where friction between the cargo and the ship's deck or structure or between cargo transport units is insufficient to avoid the risk of sliding, suitable material such as soft boards or dunnage should be used to increase friction.

2.6   Shipboard supervision

2.6.1   The principal means of preventing the improper stowage and securing of cargoes is through proper supervision of the loading operation and inspections of the stow.

2.6.2   As far as practicable, cargo spaces should be regularly inspected throughout the voyage to ensure that the cargo, vehicles and cargo transport units remain safely secured

2.7   Entering enclosed spaces

The atmosphere in any enclosed space may be incapable of supporting human life through lack of oxygen or it may contain flammable or toxic gases. The master should ensure that it is safe to enter any enclosed space.

2.8   General elements to be considered by the master

Having evaluated the risk of cargo shifting, taking into account the criteria set out in 1.5, the master should ensure, prior to loading of any cargo, cargo transport unit or vehicle, that:

.1   the deck area for their stowage is, as far as practicable, clean, dry and free from oil and grease;

.2   the cargo, cargo transport unit or vehicle appears to be in suitable condition for transport, and can be effectively secured;

.3   all necessary cargo securing equipment is on board and in good working condition; and

.4   cargo in or on cargo transport units and vehicles is, to the extent practicable, properly stowed and secured onto the unit or vehicle.

2.9   Cargo stowage and securing declaration

2.9.1   Where there is reason to suspect that a container or vehicle into which dangerous goods have been packed or loaded is not in compliance with the provisions of regulation VII/5 of SOLAS 1974, as amended, or with the provisions of parts 5 and 7, as appropriate, of the IMDG Code, or where a Container Packing Certificate/Vehicle Packing Declaration is not available, the unit should not be accepted for shipment.

2.9.2 Where practicable and feasible, road vehicles should be provided with a cargo stowage and securing declaration, stating that the cargo on the road vehicle has been properly stowed and secured for the intended sea voyage, taking into account the IMO/ILO/UN ECE Guidelines for packing of cargo transport units. An example of such a declaration is given hereunder. The Vehicle Packing Declaration, recommended by the IMDG Code (see 2.9.1), may be acceptable for this purpose.

Example

CARGO STOWAGE AND SECURING DECLARATION
Vehicle no. . . . .
Place of loading . . . .
Date of loading . . . .
Commodity(ies) . . . .
I hereby declare that the cargo on the above-mentioned vehicle has been properly stowed and secured for transport by sea, by taking into account the IMO/ILO/UN ECE Guidelines for packing of cargo transport units.
Name of signatory . . . .
Status . . . .
Place . . . . Date . . . .
Signature on behalf of the packer
Remarks: . . . .
. . . .
. . . .
. . . .
. . . .
. . . .
. . . .

Chapter 3
Standardized stowage and securing systems

3.1 Recommendations

Ships intended for the carriage of cargoes in a standardized stowage and securing system (e.g., containers, railway wagons, shipborne barges, etc.) should be:

.1 so designed and equipped that the standardized cargoes concerned can be safely stowed and secured on board under all conditions expected during the intended voyage;

.2 of a design and so equipped as to be accepted by the Administration or approved by a classification society acceptable to the Administration; and

.3 provided with adequate information, for use by the master, on the arrangements provided for the safe stowage and securing of the specific cargoes for which the ship is designed or adapted.

Chapter 4
Semi-standardized stowage and securing

4.1   Securing arrangements

4.1.1   Ships intended for the carriage of certain specific cargoes such as road vehicles, systemized cargo-carrying roll-trailers and automobiles on ro–ro ships, etc., should be provided with securing points spaced sufficiently close to each other for the intended operation of the ship and in accordance with section 4 of the guidelines for securing arrangements for the transport of road vehicles on ro–ro ships (resolution A.581(14)), as amended.

4.1.2   Road vehicles intended for transport by sea should be provided with arrangements for their safe stowage and securing, as detailed in section 5 of the annex to resolution A.581(14), as amended.

4.1.3   Roll-trailers carrying systemized cargo should be provided with arrangements for the safe stowage and securing of the vehicle and its cargo. Special consideration should be given to the height of the stow, the compactness of the stow and the effects of a high centre of gravity of the cargo.

4.2   Stowage and securing of vehicles

4.2.1   Vehicles, including roll-trailers not provided with adequate securing arrangements, should be stowed and secured in accordance with chapter 5 of this Code.

4.2.2   Ro–ro ships which do not comply with the requirements of section 4 of the annex to resolution A.581(14), as amended, or are not provided with equivalent stowage and securing means providing for an equivalent degree of safety during transport by sea should be dealt with in accordance with chapter 5 of this Code.

4.2.3   Vehicles should be stowed and secured in accordance with sections 6 and 7 of the annex to resolution A.581(14), as amended. Special consideration should be given to the stowage and securing of roll-trailers carrying systemized cargo, road tank-vehicles and portable tanks on wheels, taking into account the effects of a tank's high centre of gravity and free surface.

4.3 Acceptance of road vehicles for transport by sea on ro–ro ships

4.3.1 The master should not accept a road vehicle for transport on board his ship unless satisfied that the road vehicle is apparently suitable for the intended voyage and is provided with at least the securing points specified in section 5 of the annex to resolution A.581(14), as amended.

4.3.2 In exceptional circumstances, where there is some doubt that the recommendations of 4.3.1 can or need to be fulfilled, the master may accept the vehicle for shipment, after taking into account the condition of the vehicle and the expected nature of the intended voyage.

Chapter 5
Non-standardized stowage and securing

5.1 Recommendations

5.1.1 This chapter and the annexes provide advice of a general nature for the stowage and securing of cargoes not covered by chapters 3 and 4 of this Code and particularly specific advice for the stowage and securing of cargoes which have proved to be difficult to stow and secure on board ships.

5.1.2 The list of cargoes given in 5.3 should not be regarded as exhaustive, as there may be other cargoes which could create hazards if not properly stowed and secured.

5.2 Equivalent stowage and securing

The guidance given in the annexes provides for certain safeguards against the problems inherent in the cargoes covered. Alternative methods of stowage and securing may afford the same degree of safety. It is imperative that any alternative method chosen should provide a level of securing safety at least equivalent to that described in the resolutions, circulars and guidelines listed in the foreword to this Code.

5.3 Cargoes which have proved to be a potential source of danger

Such cargoes include:

    .1 containers when carried on deck of ships which are not specially designed and fitted for the purpose of carrying containers (annex 1);

    .2 portable tanks (tank-containers) (annex 2);

    .3 portable receptacles (annex 3);

    .4 special wheel-based (rolling) cargoes (annex 4);

    .5 heavy cargo items such as locomotives, transformers, etc. (annex 5);

.6 coiled sheet steel (annex 6);

.7 heavy metal products (annex 7);

.8 anchor chains (annex 8);

.9 metal scrap in bulk (annex 9);

.10 flexible intermediate bulk containers (FIBCs) (annex 10);

.11 logs in under-deck stow (annex 11); and

.12 unit loads (annex 12).

Chapter 6
Actions which may be taken in heavy weather

6.1 General

The purpose of this chapter is not to usurp the responsibilities of the master, but rather to offer some advice on how stresses induced by excessive accelerations caused by bad weather conditions could be avoided.

6.2 Excessive accelerations

Measures to avoid excessive accelerations are:

.1   alteration of course or speed or a combination of both;

.2   heaving to;

.3   early avoidance of areas of adverse weather and sea conditions; and

.4   timely ballasting or deballasting to improve the behaviour of the ship, taking into account the actual stability conditions (see also 7.2).

6.3 Voyage planning

One way of reducing excessive accelerations is for the master, as far as possible and practicable, to plan the voyage of the ship carefully so as to avoid areas with severe weather and sea conditions. The master should always consult the latest available weather information.

Chapter 7
Actions which may be taken once cargo has shifted

7.1   The following actions may be considered:

   .1   alterations of course to reduce accelerations;

   .2   reductions of speed to reduce accelerations and vibration;

   .3   monitoring the integrity of the ship;

   .4   restowing or resecuring the cargo and, where possible, increasing the friction; and

   .5   diversion of route in order to seek shelter or improved weather and sea conditions.

7.2   Tank ballasting or deballasting operations should be considered only if the ship has adequate stability.

Annex 1

Safe stowage and securing of containers on deck of ships which are not specially designed and fitted for the purpose of carrying containers

1   Stowage

1.1   Containers carried on deck or on hatches of such ships should preferably be stowed in the fore-and-aft direction.

1.2   Containers should not extend over the ship's sides. Adequate supports should be provided when containers overhang hatches or deck structures.

1.3   Containers should be stowed and secured so as to permit safe access for personnel in the necessary operation of the ship.

1.4   Containers should at no time overstress the deck or hatches on which they are stowed.

1.5   Bottom-tier containers, when not resting on stacking devices, should be stowed on timber of sufficient thickness, arranged in such a way as to transfer the stack load evenly on to the structure of the stowage area.

1.6   When stacking containers, use should be made of locking devices, cones, or similar stacking aids, as appropriate, between them.

1.7   When stowing containers on deck or hatches, the position and strength of the securing points should be taken into consideration.

2   Securing

2.1   All containers should be effectively secured in such a way as to protect them from sliding and tipping. Hatch covers carrying containers should be adequately secured to the ship.

2.2   Containers should be secured using one of the three methods recommended in figure 1 or methods equivalent thereto.

2.3   Lashings should preferably consist of wire ropes or chains or material with equivalent strength and elongation characteristics.

2.4   Timber shoring should not exceed 2 m in length.

2.5   Wire clips should be adequately greased, and tightened so that the dead end of the wire is visibly compressed (figure 2).

2.6   Lashings should be kept, when possible, under equal tension.

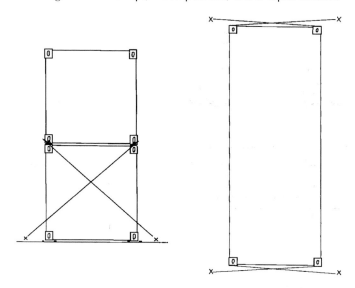

Method A – Medium-weight containers: weight of top container
not more than 70% of that of bottom container

Figure 1 – *Recommended methods of non-standardized
securing of containers*

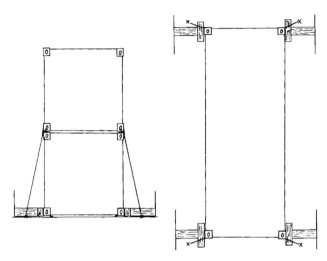

Method B – Medium-weight containers: weight of top container
may be more than 70% of that of bottom container

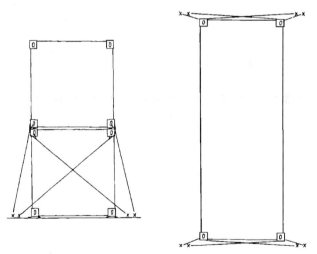

Method C – Heavyweight containers: weight of top container
may be more than 70% of that of bottom container

Figure 1 *(continued) – Recommended methods of non-standardized
securing of containers*

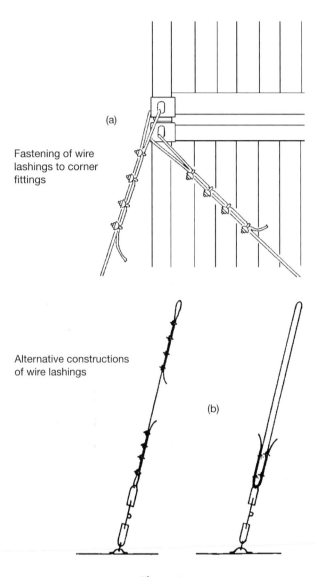

(a)

Fastening of wire
lashings to corner
fittings

Alternative constructions
of wire lashings

(b)

Figure 2

Annex 2

Safe stowage and securing of portable tanks

1   Introduction

1.1   The provisions of this annex apply to a portable tank, which in the context of this annex, means a tank which is not permanently secured on board the vessel and has a capacity of more than 450 ℓ and a shell fitted with external stabilizing members and items of service equipment and structural equipment necessary for the transport of liquids, solids or gases.

1.2   These provisions do not apply to tanks intended for the transport of liquids, solids or gases having a capacity of 450 ℓ or less.

Note: The capacity for portable tanks for gases is 1,000 ℓ or more.

2   General provisions for portable tanks

2.1   Portable tanks should be capable of being loaded and discharged without the need of removal of their structural equipment and be capable of being lifted onto and off the ship when loaded.

2.2   The applicable requirements of the International Convention for Safe Containers, 1972, as amended, should be fulfilled by any tank-container which meets the definition of a container within the terms of that Convention. Additionally, the provisions of part 6 of the IMDG Code should be met when the tank will be used for the transport of dangerous goods.

2.3   Portable tanks should not be offered for shipment in an ullage condition liable to produce an unacceptable hydraulic force due to surge within the tank.

2.4   Portable tanks for the transport of dangerous goods should be certified in accordance with the provisions of the IMDG Code by the competent approval authority or a body authorized by that authority.

3   Portable tank arrangements

3.1   The external stabilizing members of a portable tank may consist of skids or cradles and, in addition, the tank may be secured to a platform-based container. Alternatively, a tank may be fixed within a framework of ISO or non-ISO frame dimensions.

3.2 Portable tank arrangements should include fittings for lifting and securing on board.

Note: All types of the aforementioned portable tanks may be carried on multipurpose ships but need special attention for lashing and securing on board.

4   Cargo information

The master should be provided with at least the following information:

 .1 dimensions of the portable tank and commodity if non-dangerous and, if dangerous, the information required in accordance with the IMDG Code;

 .2 the gross mass of the portable tank; and

 .3 whether the portable tank is permanently secured onto a platform-based container or in a frame and whether securing points are provided.

5   Stowage

5.1 The typical distribution of accelerations of the ship should be borne in mind in deciding whether the portable tank will be stowed on or under deck.

5.2 Tanks should be stowed in the fore-and-aft direction on or under deck.

5.3 Tanks should be stowed so that they do not extend over the ship's side.

5.4 Tanks should be stowed so as to permit safe access for personnel in the necessary operation of the ship.

5.5 At no time should the tanks overstress the deck or hatches; the hatch covers should be so secured to the ship that tipping of the entire hatch cover is prevented.

6   Securing against sliding and tipping

6.1   Non-standardized portable tanks

6.1.1 The securing devices on non-standardized portable tanks and on the ship should be arranged in such a way as to withstand the transverse and longitudinal forces, which may give rise to sliding and tipping. The lashing angles against sliding should not be higher than 25° and against tipping not lower than 45° to 60° (figure 3).

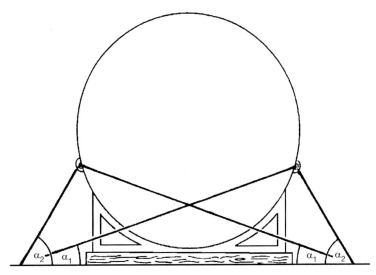

α_1 : favourable angle against sliding
α_2 : favourable angle against tipping

Figure 3 – *Securing of portable tanks with favourable lashing angles*

6.1.2 Whenever necessary, timber should be used between the deck surface and the bottom structure of the portable tank in order to increase friction. This does not apply to tanks on wooden units or with similar bottom material having a high coefficient of friction.

6.1.3 If stowage under deck is permitted, the stowage should be such that the portable non-standardized tank can be landed directly on its place and bedding.

6.1.4 Securing points on the tank should be of adequate strength and clearly marked.

Note: Securing points designed for road and rail transport may not be suitable for transport by sea.

6.1.5 Lashings attached to tanks without securing points should pass around the tank and both ends of the lashing should be secured to the same side of the tank (figure 4).

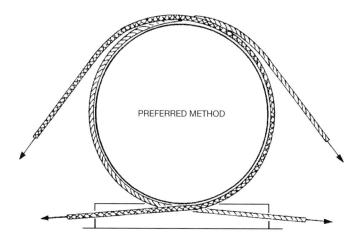

PREFERRED METHOD

Figure 4 – *Securing of portable tanks having no securing points*

6.1.6   Sufficient securing devices should be arranged in such a way that each device takes its share of the load with an adequate factor of safety.

6.1.7   The structural strength of the deck or hatch components should be taken into consideration when tanks are carried thereon and when locating and affixing the securing devices.

6.1.8   Portable tanks should be secured in such a manner that no load is imposed on the tank or fittings in excess of those for which they have been designed.

6.2   Standardized portable tanks (tank-containers)

6.2.1   Standardized portable tanks with ISO frame dimensions should be secured according to the system of lashing with which the ship is equipped, taking into consideration the height of the tank above the deck and the ullage in the tank.

7   Maintenance of securing arrangements

7.1   The integrity of the securing arrangements should be maintained throughout the voyage.

7.2   Particular attention should be paid to the need for tight lashings, grips and clips to prevent weakening through chafing.

7.3   Lashings should be regularly checked and retightened.

Annex 3

Safe stowage and securing of portable receptacles[*]

1 Introduction

A portable receptacle, in the context of these guidelines, means a receptacle not being a portable tank, which is not permanently secured on board the ship and has a capacity of 1,000 ℓ or less and has different dimensions in length, width, height and shape and which is used for the transport of gases or liquids.

2 Portable receptacles can be divided into:

.1 cylinders of different dimensions without securing points and having a capacity not exceeding 150 ℓ;

.2 receptacles of different dimensions with the exception of cylinders in conformity with 2.1 having a capacity of not less than 100 ℓ and not more than 1,000 ℓ and whether or not fitted with hoisting devices of sufficient strength; and

.3 assemblies, known as "frames", of cylinders in conformity with 2.1, the cylinders being interconnected by a manifold within the frame and held firmly together by metal fittings. The frames are equipped with securing and handling devices of sufficient strength (e.g., cylindrical receptacles are equipped with rolling hoops and receptacles are secured on skids).

3 Cargo information

3.1 The master should be provided with at least the following information:

.1 dimensions of the receptacle and commodity if non-dangerous and, if dangerous, the information as required in accordance with the IMDG Code;

.2 gross mass of the receptacles; and

.3 whether or not the receptacles are equipped with hoisting devices of sufficient strength.

---

[*] Where in this annex the term *receptacle* is used, it is meant to include both receptacles and cylinders.

4   Stowage

4.1   The typical distribution of accelerations of the ship should be borne in mind in deciding whether the receptacles should be stowed on or under deck.

4.2   The receptacles should preferably be stowed in the fore-and-aft direction on or under deck.

4.3   Receptacles should be dunnaged to prevent their resting directly on a steel deck. They should be stowed and chocked as necessary to prevent movement unless mounted in a frame as a unit. Receptacles for liquefied gases should be stowed in an upright position.

4.4   When the receptacles are stowed in an upright position, they should be stowed in a block, cribbed or boxed in with suitable and sound timber. The box or crib should be dunnaged underneath to provide clearance from a steel deck. The receptacles in a box or crib should be braced to prevent movement. The box or crib should be securely chocked and lashed to prevent movement in any direction.

5   Securing against sliding and shifting

5.1   Cylinders

Cylinders should be stowed fore-and-aft on athwartships dunnage. Where practicable, the stow should be secured by using two or more wires, laid athwartships prior to loading, and passed around the stow to securing points on opposite sides. The wires are tightened to make a compact stow by using appropriate tightening devices. During loading, wedges may be necessary to prevent cylinders rolling.

5.2   Cylinders in containers

Cylinders should, whenever practicable, be stowed upright with their valves on top and with their protective caps firmly in place. Cylinders should be adequately secured, so as to withstand the rigours of the intended voyage, by means of steel strapping or equivalent means led to lashing points on the container floor. When cylinders cannot be stowed upright in a closed container, they should be carried in an open-top or a platform-based container.

5.3 Receptacles

Securing of receptacles stowed on or under deck should be as follows:

.1 lashings should be positioned as shown in figure 5;

.2 where possible, the hoisting devices on receptacles should be used to lash them; and

.3 at regular times the lashings should be checked and retightened.

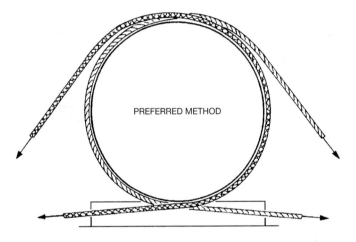

PREFERRED METHOD

Figure 5 – *Securing of receptacles having no securing points*

Annex 4

Safe stowage and securing of wheel-based (rolling) cargoes

1   Introduction

Wheel-based cargoes, in the context of these guidelines, are all cargoes which are provided with wheels or tracks, including those which are used for the stowage and transport of other cargoes, except trailers and road-trains (covered by chapter 4 of this Code), but including buses, military vehicles with or without tracks, tractors, earth-moving equipment, roll-trailers, etc.

2   General recommendations

2.1   The cargo spaces in which wheel-based cargo is to be stowed should be dry, clean and free from grease and oil.

2.2   Wheel-based cargoes should be provided with adequate and clearly marked securing points or other equivalent means of sufficient strength to which lashings may be applied.

2.3   Wheel-based cargoes which are not provided with securing points should have those places where lashings may be applied clearly marked.

2.4   Wheel-based cargoes which are not provided with rubber wheels or tracks with friction-increasing lower surface should always be stowed on wooden dunnage or other friction-increasing material such as soft boards, rubber mats, etc.

2.5   When in stowage position, the brakes of a wheel-based unit, if so equipped, should be set.

2.6   Wheel-based cargoes should be secured to the ship by lashings made of material having strength and elongation characteristics at least equivalent to steel chain or wire.

2.7   Where possible, wheel-based cargoes, carried as part cargo, should be stowed close to the ship's side or in stowage positions which are provided with sufficient securing points of sufficient strength, or be block-stowed from side to side of the cargo space.

2.8   To prevent any lateral shifting of wheel-based cargoes not provided with adequate securing points, such cargoes should, where practicable, be stowed close to the ship's side and close to each other, or be blocked off by other suitable cargo units such as loaded containers, etc.

2.9   To prevent the shifting of wheel-based cargoes, it is, where practicable, preferable to stow those cargoes in a fore-and-aft direction rather than athwartships. If wheel-based cargoes are inevitably stowed athwartships, additional securing of sufficient strength may be necessary.

2.10   The wheels of wheel-based cargoes should be blocked to prevent shifting.

2.11   Cargoes stowed on wheel-based units should be adequately secured to stowage platforms or, where provided with suitable means, to its sides. Any movable external components attached to a wheel-based unit, such as derricks, arms or turrets, should be adequately locked or secured in position.

Annex 5

Safe stowage and securing of heavy cargo items such as locomotives, transformers, etc.

1 Cargo information

The master should be provided with sufficient information on any heavy cargo offered for shipment so that he can properly plan its stowage and securing; the information should at least include the following:

.1 gross mass;

.2 principal dimensions with drawings or pictorial descriptions, if possible;

.3 location of the centre of gravity;

.4 bedding areas and particular bedding precautions if applicable;

.5 lifting points or slinging positions; and

.6 securing points, where provided, including details of their strength.

2 Location of stowage

2.1 When considering the location for stowing a heavy cargo item, the typical distribution of accelerations on the ship should be kept in mind:

.1 lower accelerations occur in the midship sections and below the weather deck; and

.2 higher accelerations occur in the end sections and above the weather deck.

2.2 When heavy items are to be stowed on deck, the expected "weather side" of the particular voyage should be taken into account if possible.

2.3 Heavy items should preferably be stowed in the fore-and-aft direction.

3 Distribution of weight

The weight of the item should be distributed in such a way as to avoid undue stress on the ship's structure. Particularly with the carriage of heavy items on decks or hatch covers, suitable beams of timber or steel of adequate strength should be used to transfer the weight of the item onto the ship's structure.

4 Cargo stowed in open containers, on platforms or platform-based containers

4.1   While the stowage and securing of open containers, ISO platforms or platform-based containers (flatracks) on a containership or a ship fitted or adapted for the carriage of containers should follow the information for that system, the stowage and securing of the cargo in such containers should be carried out in accordance with the IMO/ILO/ UN ECE Guidelines for packing of cargo transport units.

4.2   When heavy cargo items are carried on ISO platforms or platform-based containers (flatracks) the provisions of this annex should be followed. Additionally, the following items should be taken into account:

.1   The ISO standard platform, etc., used should be of a suitable type with regard to strength and MSL of the securing points.

.2   The weight of the heavy cargo item should be properly distributed.

.3   Where deemed necessary, the heavy cargo item(s) carried on ISO standard platform(s) or platform-based containers, etc., should not only be secured to the platform(s) or platform-based containers, etc., but also to neighbouring platform(s), etc., or to securing points located at fixed structure of the ship. The elasticity of the last-mentioned lashings should be sufficiently in line with the overall elasticity of the stowage block underneath the heavy cargo item(s) in order to avoid overloading those lashings.

5 Securing against sliding and tipping

5.1   Whenever possible, timber should be used between the stowage surface and the bottom of the unit in order to increase friction. This does not apply to items on wooden cradles or on rubber tyres or with similar bottom material having a high coefficient of friction.

5.2   The securing devices should be arranged in a way to withstand transverse and longitudinal forces which may give rise to sliding or tipping.

5.3 The optimum lashing angle against sliding is about 25°, while the optimum lashing angle against tipping is generally found between 45° and 60° (figure 6).

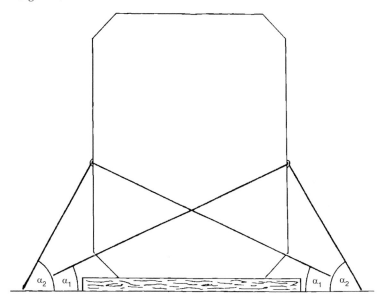

α₁ : favourable angle against sliding
α₂ : favourable angle against tipping

Figure 6 – *Principles of securing heavy items against sliding and tipping*

5.4 If a heavy cargo item has been dragged into position on greased skid boards or other means to reduce friction, the number of lashings used to prevent sliding should be increased accordingly.

5.5 If, owing to circumstances, lashings can be set at large angles only, sliding must be prevented by timber shoring, welded fittings or other appropriate means. Any welding should be carried out in accordance with accepted hot-work procedures.

6   Securing against heavy seas on deck

Whilst it is recognized that securing cargo items against heavy seas on deck is difficult, all efforts should be made to secure such items and their supports to withstand such impact and special means of securing may have to be considered.

7 Heavy cargo items projecting over the ship's side

Items projecting over the ship's side should be additionally secured by lashings acting in longitudinal and vertical directions.

8 Attachment of lashings to heavy cargo items

8.1 If lashings are to be attached to securing points on the item, these securing points should be of adequate strength and clearly marked. It should be borne in mind that securing points designed for road or rail transport may not be suitable for securing the items on board ship.

8.2 Lashings attached to items without securing points should pass around the item, or a rigid part thereof, and both ends of the lashing should be secured to the same side of the unit (figure 7).

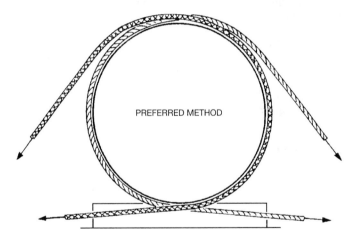

PREFERRED METHOD

Figure 7 – *Principle of securing heavy items having no suitable securing points*

9 Composition and application of securing devices

9.1 Securing devices should be assembled so that each component is of equal strength.

9.2 Connecting elements and tightening devices should be used in the correct way. Consideration should be given to any reduction of the strength of the lashings during the voyage through corrosion, fatigue or mechanical deterioration and should be compensated by using stronger securing material.

9.3   Particular attention should be paid to the correct use of wire, grips and clips. The saddle portion of the clip should be applied to the live load segment and the U-bolt to the dead or shortened end segment.

9.4   Securing devices should be arranged in such a way that each device takes its share of load according to its strength.

9.5   Mixed securing arrangements of devices with different strength and elongation characteristics should be avoided.

10   Maintenance of securing arrangements

10.1   The integrity of the securing arrangements should be maintained throughout the voyage.

10.2   Particular attention should be paid to the need for tight lashings, grips and clips and to prevent weakening through chafing. Timber cradles, beddings and shorings should be checked.

10.3   Greasing the thread of clips and turnbuckles increases their holding capacity and prevents corrosion.

11   Securing calculation

Where necessary, the securing arrangements for heavy cargo items should be verified by an appropriate calculation in accordance with annex 13 to the Code.

Annex 6

Safe stowage and securing of coiled sheet steel

1   General

1.1   This annex deals only with coiled sheet steel stowed on the round. Vertical stowage is not dealt with because this type of stowage does not create any special securing problems.

1.2   Normally, coils of sheet steel have a gross mass in excess of 10 tonnes each.

2   Coils

2.1   Coils should be given bottom stow and, whenever possible, be stowed in regular tiers from side to side of the ship.

2.2   Coils should be stowed on dunnage laid athwartships. Coils should be stowed with their axes in the fore-and-aft direction. Each coil should be stowed against its neighbour. Wedges should be used as stoppers when necessary during loading and discharging to prevent shifting (figures 8 and 9).

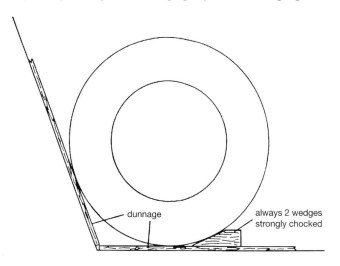

Figure 8 – *Principle of dunnaging and wedging coils*

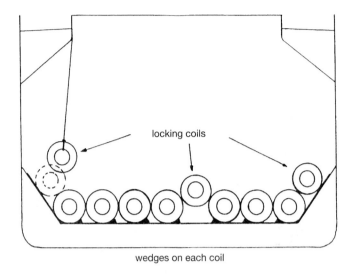

wedges on each coil

Figure 9 – *Inserting of locking coils*

2.3   The final coil in each row should normally rest on the two adjacent coils. The mass of this coil will lock the other coils in the row.

2.4   If it is necessary to load a second tier over the first, then the coils should be stowed in between the coils of the first tier (figure 9).

2.5   Any void space between coils in the topmost tier should be adequately secured (figure 10).

3   Lashings

3.1   The objective is to form one large, immovable block of coils in the hold by lashing them together. In general, strip coils in three end rows in the top tier should be lashed. To prevent fore-and-aft shifting in the top tier of bare-wound coils, group-lashing should not be applied due to their fragile nature; the end row of a top tier should be secured by dunnage and wires, which are to be tightened from side to side, and by additional wires to the bulkhead. When coils are fully loaded over the entire bottom space and are well shored, no lashings are required except for locking coils (figures 11, 12, and 13).

3.2   The lashings can be of a conventional type using wire, steel band or any equivalent means.

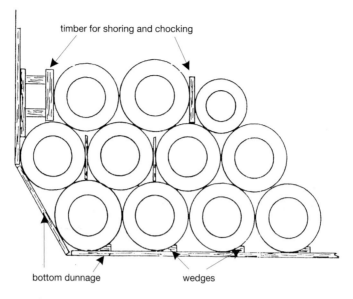

timber for shoring and chocking

bottom dunnage   wedges

Figure 10 – *Shoring and chocking in voids between coils*

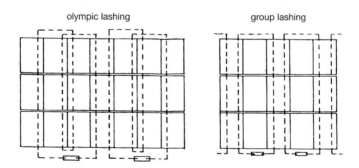

olympic lashing   group lashing

Figure 11 – *Securing of top tier against fore-and-aft shifting (view from top)*

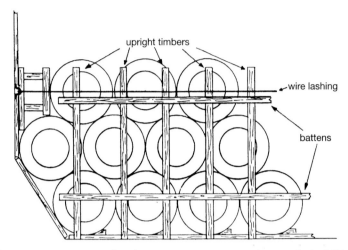

Figure 12 – *Securing of end row in top tier against fore-and-aft shifting*

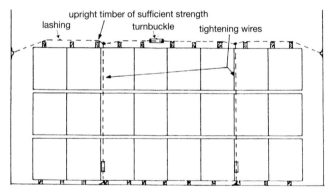

Figure 13 – *Securing of end row in top tier against fore-and-aft shifting (view from top)*

3.3   Conventional lashings should consist of wires having sufficient tensile strength. The first tier should be chocked. It should be possible to retighten the lashings during the voyage (figures 12 and 13).

3.4   Wire lashings should be protected against damage from sharp edges.

3.5   If there are few coils, or a single coil only, they should be adequately secured to the ship, by placing them in cradles, by wedging, or by shoring and then lashing to prevent transverse and longitudinal movement.

3.6   Coils carried in containers, railway wagons and road vehicles should be stowed in cradles or specially made beds and should be prevented from moving by adequate securing.

Annex 7

Safe stowage and securing of heavy metal products

1 General

1.1 Heavy metal products in the context of this Code include any heavy item made of metal, such as bars, pipes, rods, plates, wire coils, etc.

1.2 The transport of heavy metal products by sea exposes the ship to the following principal hazards:

.1 overstressing of the ship's structure if the permissible hull stress or permissible deck loading is exceeded;

.2 overstressing of the ship's structure as a result of a short roll period caused by excessive metacentric height; and

.3 cargo shifting because of inadequate securing resulting in a loss of stability or damage to the hull or both.

2 Recommendations

2.1 The cargo spaces in which heavy metal products are to be stowed should be clean, dry and free from grease and oil.

2.2 The cargo should be so distributed as to avoid undue hull stress.

2.3 The permissible deck and tank top loading should not be exceeded.

2.4 The following measures should be taken when stowing and securing heavy metal products:

.1 cargo items should be stowed compactly from one side of the ship to the other, leaving no voids between them and using timber blocks between items if necessary;

.2 cargo should be stowed level whenever possible and practicable;

.3 the surface of the cargo should be secured; and

.4 the shoring should be made of strong, non-splintering wood and adequately sized to withstand the acceleration forces. One shoring should be applied to every frame of the ship but at intervals of not less than 1 m.

2.5   In the case of thin plates and small parcels, alternate fore-and-aft and athwartships stowage has proved satisfactory. The friction should be increased by using sufficient dry dunnage or other material between the different layers.

2.6   Pipes, rails, rolled sections, billets, etc., should be stowed in the fore-and-aft direction to avoid damage to the sides of the ship if the cargo shifts.

2.7   The cargo, and especially the topmost layer, can be secured by:

    .1   having other cargo stowed on top of it; or

    .2   lashing by wire, chocking off or similar means.

2.8   Whenever heavy metal products are not stowed from side to side of the ship, special care should be taken to secure such stowages adequately.

2.9   Whenever the surface of the cargo is to be secured, the lashings should be independent of each other, exert vertical pressure on the surface of the cargo, and be so positioned that no part of the cargo is unsecured.

3   Wire coils

3.1   Wire coils should be stowed flat so that each coil rests against an adjacent coil. The coils in successive tiers should be stowed so that each coil overlaps the coils below.

3.2   Wire coils should be tightly stowed together and substantial securing arrangements should be used. Where voids between coils are unavoidable or where there are voids at the sides or ends of the cargo space, the stow should be adequately secured.

3.3   When securing wire coils stowed on their sides in several layers like barrels, it is essential to remember that, unless the top layer is secured, the coils lying in the stow can be forced out of the stow by the coils below on account of the ship's motions.

Annex 8

Safe stowage and securing of anchor chains

1   General

1.1   Anchor chains for ships and offshore structures are usually carried in bundles or in continuous lengths.

1.2   Provided certain safety measures are followed prior to, during and after stowage, anchor chains may be lowered directly onto the place of stowage in bundles without further handling or stowed longitudinally either along the ship's entire cargo space or part thereof.

1.3   If the cargo plans given in the ship's documentation contain no specific requirements, the cargo should be distributed over the lower hold and 'tween-decks in such a way that stability values thus obtained will guarantee adequate stability.

2   Recommendations

2.1   Cargo spaces in which chains are stowed should be clean and free from oil and grease.

2.2   Chains should only be stowed on surfaces which are permanently covered either by wooden ceiling or by sufficient layers of dunnage or other suitable friction-increasing materials. Chains should never be stowed directly on metal surfaces.

3   Stowage and securing of chains in bundles

3.1   Chains in bundles, which are lifted directly onto their place of stowage without further handling, should be left with their lifting wires attached and should preferably be provided with additional wires around the bundles for lashing purposes.

3.2   It is not necessary to separate layers of chain with friction-increasing material such as dunnage because chain bundles will grip each other. The top layer of chain bundles should be secured to both sides of the ship by suitable lashings. Bundles may be lashed independently or in a group, using the lifting wires.

4 Stowage and securing of chains which are stowed longitudinally

4.1 Stowage of each layer of chain should, whenever possible and practicable, commence and terminate close to the ship's side. Care should be taken to achieve a tight stow.

4.2 It is not necessary to separate layers of chain with friction-increasing material such as dunnage because chain layers will grip each other.

4.3 Bearing in mind the expected weather and sea conditions, the length and nature of the voyage and the nature of the cargo to be stowed on top of the chain, the top layer of each stow should be secured by lashings of adequate strength crossing the stow at suitable intervals and thus holding down the entire stow.

Annex 9

Safe stowage and securing of metal scrap in bulk

1 Introduction

1.1 This annex deals with the stowage of metal scrap which is difficult to stow compactly because of its size, shape and mass, but does not apply to metal scrap such as metal borings, shavings or turnings, the carriage of which is addressed by the Code of Safe Practice for Solid Bulk Cargoes.

1.2 The hazards involved in transporting metal scrap include:

- **.1** shifting of the stow which in turn can cause a list;
- **.2** shifting of individual heavy pieces which can rupture the side plating below the waterline and give rise to serious flooding;
- **.3** excessive loading on tank tops or 'tween-decks; and
- **.4** violent rolling caused by excessive metacentric height.

2 Recommendations

2.1 Before loading, the lower battens of the spar ceiling should be protected by substantial dunnage to reduce damage and to prevent heavy and sharp pieces of scrap coming in contact with the ship's side plating. Air and sounding pipes, and bilge and ballast lines protected only by wooden boards, should be similarly protected.

2.2 When loading, care should be taken to ensure that the first loads are not dropped from a height which could damage the tank tops.

2.3 If light and heavy scrap is to be stowed in the same cargo space, the heavy scrap should be loaded first. Scrap should never be stowed on top of metal turnings, or similar forms of waste metal.

2.4 Scrap should be compactly and evenly stowed with no voids or unsupported faces of loosely held scrap.

2.5 Heavy pieces of scrap, which could cause damage to the side plating or end bulkheads if they were to move, should be overstowed or secured by suitable lashings. The use of shoring is unlikely to be effective because of the nature of the scrap.

2.6 Care should be taken to avoid excessive loading on tank tops and decks.

Annex 10

Safe stowage and securing of flexible intermediate bulk containers

1   Introduction

A flexible intermediate bulk container (FIBC), in the context of these guidelines, means a flexible portable packaging to be used for the transport of solids with a capacity of not more than 3 m^3 (3,000 ℓ) designed for mechanical handling and tested for its satisfactory resistance to transport and transport stresses in a one-way type or multi-purpose design.

2   Cargo information

The master should at least be provided with the following information:

.1   the total number of FIBCs and the commodity to be loaded;

.2   the dimensions of the FIBCs;

.3   the total gross mass of the FIBCs;

.4   one-way type or multi-purpose design; and

.5   the kind of hoisting (one hook or more hooks to be used).

3   Recommendations

3.1   The ideal ship for the carriage of FIBCs is one with wide hatches so that the FIBCs can be landed directly in the stowage positions without the need for shifting.

3.2   The cargo spaces should, where practicable, be rectangular in shape and free of obstructions.

3.3   The stowage space should be clean, dry and free from oil and nails.

3.4   When FIBCs have to be stowed in deep hatch wings, easy access and sufficient manoeuvring space for suitably adapted fork-lift trucks should be available.

3.5   When FIBCs are stowed in the hatchway only, the space in the wings and the forward and aft end of the cargo space should be loaded with other suitable cargo or blocked off in such a way that the FIBCs are adequately supported.

4   Stowage

4.1   The typical distribution of the accelerations of the ship should be kept in mind when FIBCs are loaded.

4.2   The width of the ship divided by the width of the FIBC will give the number of FIBCs which can be stowed athwartships and the void space left. If there will be a void space, the stowage of the FIBCs should start from both sides to the centre, so that any void space will be in the centre of the hatchway.

4.3   FIBCs should be stowed as close as possible against each other and any void space should be chocked off.

4.4   The next layers should be stowed in a similar way so that the FIBCs fully cover the FIBCs underneath. If in this layer a void space is left, it should also be chocked off in the centre of the hatchway.

4.5   When there is sufficient room in the hatchway on top of the layers underneath to stow another layer, it should be established whether the coamings can be used as bulkheads. If not, measures should be taken to prevent the FIBCs shifting to the open space in the wings. Otherwise, the FIBCs should be stowed from one coaming to another. In both cases any void space should be in the centre and should be chocked off.

4.6   Chocking off is necessary in all cases to prevent shifting of the FIBCs to either side and to prevent a list of the ship developing in rough weather (figure 14).

5   Securing

5.1   In cases where only a part of a 'tween-deck or lower hold is used for the stowage of FIBCs, measures should be taken to prevent the FIBCs from shifting. These measures should include sufficient gratings or plywood sheets placed against the FIBCs and the use of wire lashings from side to side to secure the FIBC cargo.

5.2   The wire lashings and plywood sheets used for securing should be regularly checked, in particular before and after rough weather, and retightened if necessary.

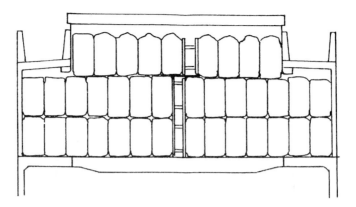

Figure 14 – *Stowage of FIBCs with chocked void spaces in the centre of the stowage area*

Annex 11

*General guidelines for the under-deck
stowage of logs*

1   Introduction

The purpose of this annex is to recommend safe practices for the under-deck stowage of logs and other operational safety measures designed to ensure the safe transport of such cargoes.

2   Prior to loading:

   .1   each cargo space configuration (length, breadth and depth), the cubic bale capacity of the respective cargo spaces, the various lengths of logs to be loaded, the cubic volume (log average), and the capacity of the gear to be used to load the logs should be determined;

   .2   using the above information, a pre-stow plan should be developed to allow the maximum utilization of the available space; the better the under-deck stowage, the more cargo can safely be carried on deck;

   .3   the cargo spaces and related equipment should be examined to determine whether the condition of structural members, framework and equipment could affect the safe carriage of the log cargo. Any damage discovered during such an examination should be repaired in an appropriate manner;

   .4   the bilge suction screens should be examined to ensure they are clean, effective and properly maintained to prevent the admission of debris into the bilge piping system;

   .5   the bilge wells should be free of extraneous material such as wood bark and wood splinters;

   .6   the capacity of the bilge pumping system should be ascertained. A properly maintained and operating system is crucial for the safety of the ship. A portable dewatering pump of sufficient capacity and lift will provide additional insurance against a clogged bilge line;

   .7   side sparring, pipe guards, etc., designed to protect internal hull members should be in place; and

.8 the master should ensure that the opening and closing of any high ballast dump valves are properly recorded in the ship's log. Given that such high ballast tanks are necessary to facilitate loading and bearing in mind regulation 22(1) of the International Convention on Load Lines, 1966, which requires a screw-down valve fitted in gravity overboard drain lines, the master should ensure that the dump valves are properly monitored to preclude the accidental re-admission of water into these tanks. Leaving these tanks open to the sea could lead to an apparently inexplicable list, a shift of deck cargo, and potential capsize.

3   During loading operations:

.1 each lift of logs should be hoisted aboard the ship in close proximity to the ship to minimize any potential swinging of the lift;

.2 the possibility of damage to the ship and the safety of those who work in the cargo spaces should be considered. The logs should not be swinging when lowered into the space. The hatch coaming should be used, as necessary, to eliminate any swinging of the logs by gently resting the load against the inside of the coaming, or on it, prior to lowering;

.3 the logs should be stowed compactly, thereby eliminating as many voids as is practicable. The amount and the vertical centre of gravity of the logs stowed under deck will govern the amount of cargo that can be safely stowed on deck. In considering this principle, the heaviest logs should be loaded first into the cargo spaces;

.4 logs should generally be stowed compactly in a fore-and-aft direction, with the longer lengths towards the forward and aft areas of the space. If there is a void in the space between the fore and aft lengths, it should be filled with logs stowed athwartships so as to fill in the void across the breadth of the spaces as completely as the length of the logs permits;

.5 where the logs in the spaces can only be stowed fore-and-aft in one length, any remaining void forward or aft should be filled with logs stowed athwartships so as to fill in the void across the breadth of the space as completely as the length of the logs permits;

.6 athwartship voids should be filled tier by tier as loading progresses;

   .7   butt ends of the logs should be alternately reversed to achieve a more level stowage, except where excess sheer on the inner bottom is encountered;

   .8   extreme pyramiding of logs should be avoided to the greatest extent possible. If the breadth of the space is greater than the breadth of the hatch opening, pyramiding may be avoided by sliding fore-and-aft loaded logs into the ends of the port and starboard sides of the space. This sliding of logs into the ends of the port and starboard sides of the space should commence early in the loading process (after reaching a height of approximately 2 m above the inner bottom) and should continue throughout the loading process;

   .9   it may be necessary to use loose tackle to manoeuvre heavy logs into the under-deck areas clear of the hatchways. Blocks, purchases and other loose tackle should be attached to suitably reinforced fixtures such as eyebolts or padeyes provided for this purpose. However, if this procedure is followed, care should be taken to avoid overloading the gear;

   .10   a careful watch by ship's personnel should be maintained throughout the loading to ensure no structural damage occurs. Any damage which affects the seaworthiness of the ship should be repaired;

   .11   when the logs are stowed to a height of about 1 m below the forward or aft athwartship hatch coaming, the size of the lift of logs should be reduced to facilitate stowing of the remaining area; and

   .12   logs in the hatch coaming area should be stowed as compactly as possible to maximum capacity.

4   After loading, the ship should be thoroughly examined to ascertain its structural condition. Bilges should be sounded to verify the ship's watertight integrity.

5   During the voyage:

   .1   the ship's heeling angle and rolling period should be checked, in a seaway, on a regular basis;

   .2   wedges, wastes, hammers and portable pump, if provided, should be stored in an easily accessible place; and

.3 the master or a responsible officer should ensure that it is safe to enter an enclosed cargo space by:

    .3.1 ensuring that the space has been thoroughly ventilated by natural or mechanical means;

    .3.2 testing the atmosphere of the space at different levels for oxygen deficiency and harmful vapour where suitable instruments are available; and

    .3.3 requiring self-contained breathing apparatus to be worn by all persons entering the space where there is any doubt as to the adequacy of ventilation or testing before entry.

Annex 12

Safe stowage and securing of unit loads

1   Introduction

Unit load for the purposes of this annex means that a number of packages are either:

.1   placed or stacked, and secured by strapping, shrink-wrapping or other suitable means, on a load board such as a pallet; or

.2   placed in a protective outer packaging such as a pallet box; or

.3   permanently secured together in a sling.

Note: A single large package such as a portable tank or receptacle, intermediate bulk container or freight container is excluded from the recommendations of this annex.

2   Cargo information

The master should be provided with at least the following information:

.1   the total number of unit loads and commodity to be loaded;

.2   the type of strapping or wrapping used;

.3   the dimensions of a unit load in metres;

.4   the gross mass of a unit load in kilograms; and

.5   relevant examination certificates for pre-slung slings around cargo units. The slings should be identified by specific means, e.g., colour coding, batch numbers or otherwise.

3   Recommendations

3.1   The cargo spaces of the ship in which unit loads will be stowed should be clean, dry and free from oil and grease.

3.2   The decks, including the tank top, should be flush all over.

3.3   The cargo spaces should preferably be of a rectangular shape, horizontally and vertically. Cargo spaces of another shape in forward holds or in 'tween-decks should be transformed into a rectangular shape both athwartships and longitudinally by the use of suitable timber (figure 15).

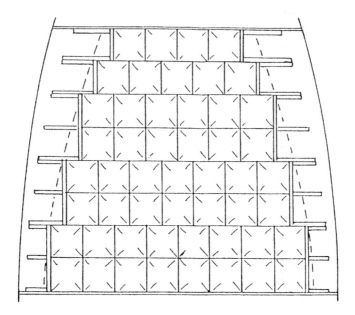

Figure 15 – *Stowage and chocking of unit loads
in a tapered stowage area (view from top)*

4   Stowage

4.1   The unit loads should be stowed in such a way that securing, if needed, can be performed on all sides of the stow.

4.2   The unit loads should be stowed without any void space between the loads and the ship's sides to prevent the unit loads from racking.

4.3   When unit loads have to be stowed on top of each other, attention should be paid to the strength of pallets and the shape and the condition of the unit loads.

4.4   Precautions should be taken when unit loads are mechanically handled to avoid damaging the unit loads.

5   Securing

Block stowage should be ensured and no void space be left between the unit loads.

6   Securing when stowed athwartships

6.1   When unit loads are stowed in a lower hold or in a 'tween-deck against a bulkhead from side to side, gratings or plywood sheets should be positioned vertically against the stack of the unit loads. Wire lashings should be fitted from side to side keeping the gratings or plywood sheets tight against the stow.

6.2   Additionally, lashing wires can be fitted at different spacing from the bulkhead over the stow to the horizontally placed wire lashings in order to further tighten the stow.

7   Stowage in a wing of a cargo space   and free at two sides

When unit loads are stowed in the forward or after end of a cargo space and the possibility of shifting in two directions exists, gratings or plywood sheets should be positioned vertically to the stack faces of the unit loads of the non-secured sides of the stow. Wire lashings should be taken around the stow from the wings to the bulkhead. Where the wires can damage the unit loads (particularly on the corners of the stow), gratings or plywood sheets should be positioned in such a way that no damage can occur on corners.

8   Stowage free at three sides

When unit loads are stowed against the ship's sides in such a way that shifting is possible from three sides, gratings or plywood sheets should be positioned vertically against the stack faces of the unit loads. Special attention should be paid to the corners of the stow to prevent damage to the unit loads by the wire lashings. Wire lashing at different heights should tighten the stow together with the gratings or plywood sheets at the sides (figure 16).

9   General

9.1   Instead of gratings or plywood sheets, other possibilities are the use of aluminium stanchions or battens of sufficient strength.

9.2   During the voyage the wire lashings should be regularly inspected and slack wires should be retightened if necessary. In particular, after rough weather, wire lashings should be checked and retightened if necessary.

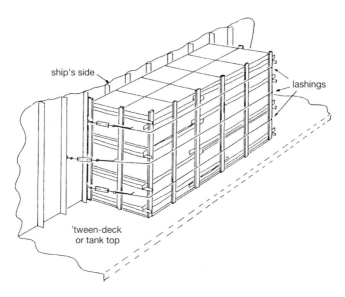

Figure 16 – *Securing of units stowed at the ship's side*

Annex 13

Methods to assess the efficiency of securing arrangements for non-standardized cargo

1 Scope of application

The methods described in this annex should be applied to non-standardized cargoes, but not to containers on containerships.

Very heavy units as carried under the provisions of chapter 1.8 of the Code of Safe Practice for Cargo Stowage and Securing (the Code) and those items for which exhaustive advice on stowage and securing is given in the annexes to the Code should be excluded. All lashing assemblies used in the application of the methods described in this annex must be attached to fixed securing points or strong supporting structures marked on the cargo unit or advised as being suitable, or taken as a loop around the unit with both ends secured to the same side as shown in annex 5, figure 7 of the Code. Lashings going over the top of the cargo unit, which have no defined securing direction but only act to increase friction by their pre-tension, cannot be credited in the evaluation of securing arrangements under this annex.

Nothing in this annex should be read to exclude the use of computer software, provided the output achieves design parameters which meet the minimum safety factors applied in this annex.

The application of the methods described in this annex is supplementary to the principles of good seamanship and shall not replace experience in stowage and securing practice.

2 Purpose of the methods

The methods should:

.1 provide guidance for the preparation of the Cargo Securing Manual and the examples therein;

.2 assist ship's staff in assessing the securing of cargo units not covered by the Cargo Securing Manual;

.3 assist qualified shore personnel in assessing the securing of cargo units not covered by the Cargo Securing Manual; and

.4 serve as a reference for maritime and port-related education and training.

3 Presentation of the methods

The methods are presented in a universally applicable and flexible way. It is recommended that designers of Cargo Securing Manuals convert this presentation into a form suiting the particular ship, its securing equipment and the cargo carried. This form may consist of applicable diagrams, tables or calculated examples.

4 Strength of securing equipment

4.1 Manufacturers of securing equipment should at least supply information on the nominal breaking strength of the equipment in kilonewtons (kN).[*]

4.2 "Maximum securing load" (MSL) is a term used to define the load capacity for a device used to secure cargo to a ship. "Safe Working Load" (SWL) may be substituted for MSL for securing purposes, provided this is equal to or exceeds the strength defined by MSL.

The MSLs for different securing devices are given in table 1 if not given under 4.3.

The MSL of timber should be taken as 0.3 kN/cm^2 normal to the grain.

Table 1– *Determination of MSL from breaking strength*

Material	MSL
Shackles, rings, deckeyes, turnbuckles of mild steel	50% of breaking strength
Fibre rope	33% of breaking strength
Web lashing	50% of breaking strength
Wire rope (single use)	80% of breaking strength
Wire rope (re-useable)	30% of breaking strength
Steel band (single use)	70% of breaking strength
Chains	50% of breaking strength

4.3 For particular securing devices (e.g., fibre straps with tensioners or special equipment for securing containers), a permissible working load may be prescribed and marked by authority. This should be taken as the MSL.

4.4 When the components of a lashing device are connected in series (for example, a wire to a shackle to a deckeye), the minimum MSL in the series shall apply to that device.

---

[*] 1 kN ≈ 100 kg.

5   Rule-of-thumb method

5.1   The total of the MSL values of the securing devices on each side of a unit of cargo (port as well as starboard) should equal the weight of the unit.[*]

5.2   This method, which implies a transverse acceleration of $1g$ (9.81 m/s^2), applies to nearly any size of ship, regardless of the location of stowage, stability and loading condition, season and area of operation. The method, however, takes into account neither the adverse effects of lashing angles and non-homogeneous distribution of forces among the securing devices nor the favourable effect of friction.

5.3   Transverse lashing angles to the deck should not be greater than 60° and it is important that adequate friction is provided by the use of suitable material. Additional lashings at angles of greater than 60° may be desirable to prevent tipping but are not to be counted in the number of lashings under the rule-of-thumb.

6   Safety factor

When using balance calculation methods for assessing the strength of the securing devices, a safety factor is used to take account of the possibility of uneven distribution of forces among the devices or reduced capability due to the improper assembly of the devices or other reasons. This safety factor is used in the formula to derive the calculated strength (*CS*) from the MSL and shown in the relevant method used.

$$CS = \frac{MSL}{\text{safety factor}}$$

Notwithstanding the introduction of such a safety factor, care should be taken to use securing elements of similar material and length in order to provide a uniform elastic behaviour within the arrangement.

7   Advanced calculation method

7.1   Assumption of external forces

External forces to a cargo unit in longitudinal, transverse and vertical directions should be obtained using the formula:

$$F_{(x,y,z)} = m \cdot a_{(x,y,z)} + F_{w(x,y)} + F_{s(x,y)}$$

---

[*] The weight of the unit should be taken in kN.

where

$F_{(x,y,z)}$ = longitudinal, transverse and vertical forces

m = mass of the unit

$a_{(x,y,z)}$ = longitudinal, transverse and vertical accelerations (see table 2)

$F_{w(x,y)}$ = longitudinal and transverse forces by wind pressure

$F_{s(x,y)}$ = longitudinal and transverse forces by sea sloshing.

The basic acceleration data are presented in table 2.

Table 2 – *Basic acceleration data*

Transverse acceleration a_y in m/s²									Longitudinal acceleration a_x in m/s²
on deck, high	7.1 6.9 6.8 6.7 6.7 6.8 6.9 7.1 7.4								3.8
on deck, low	6.5 6.3 6.1 6.1 6.1 6.1 6.3 6.5 6.7								2.9
'tween-deck	5.9 5.6 5.5 5.4 5.4 5.5 5.6 5.9 6.2								2.0
lower hold	5.5 5.3 5.1 5.0 5.0 5.1 5.3 5.5 5.9								1.5
	0 0.1 0.2 0.3 0.4 0.5 0.6 0.7 0.8 0.9 *L*								
Vertical acceleration a_z in m/s²									
7.6 6.2 5.0 4.3 4.3 5.0 6.2 7.6 9.2									

Remarks:

The given transverse acceleration figures include components of gravity, pitch and heave parallel to the deck. The given vertical acceleration figures do not include the static weight component.

The basic acceleration data are to be considered as valid under the following operational conditions:

.1   Operation in unrestricted area;

.2   Operation during the whole year;

.3   Duration of the voyage is 25 days;

.4   Length of ship is 100 m;

.5   Service speed is 15 knots;

.6 $B/GM \geq 13$ (B = breadth of ship, GM = metacentric height).

For operation in a restricted area, reduction of these figures may be considered, taking into account the season of the year and the duration of the voyage.

For ships of a length other than 100 m and a service speed other than 15 knots, the acceleration figures should be corrected by a factor given in table 3.

Table 3 – *Correction factors for length and speed*

Length (m) Speed (kn)	50	60	70	80	90	100	120	140	160	180	200
9	1.20	1.09	1.00	0.92	0.85	0.79	0.70	0.63	0.57	0.53	0.49
12	1.34	1.22	1.12	1.03	0.96	0.90	0.79	0.72	0.65	0.60	0.56
15	1.49	1.36	1.24	1.15	1.07	1.00	0.89	0.80	0.73	0.68	0.63
18	1.64	1.49	1.37	1.27	1.18	1.10	0.98	0.89	0.82	0.76	0.71
21	1.78	1.62	1.49	1.38	1.29	1.21	1.08	0.98	0.90	0.83	0.78
24	1.93	1.76	1.62	1.50	1.40	1.31	1.17	1.07	0.98	0.91	0.85

For length/speed combinations not directly tabulated, the following formula may be used to obtain the correction factor with v = speed in knots and L = length between perpendiculars in metres:

$$\text{correction factor} = (0.345 \cdot v/\sqrt{L}) + (58.62 \cdot L - 1034.5)/L^2$$

This formula shall not be used for ship lengths less than 50 m or more than 300 m.

In addition, for ships with B/GM less than 13, the transverse acceleration figures should be corrected by a factor given in table 4.

Table 4 – *Correction factors for B/GM < 13*

B/GM	7	8	9	10	11	12	13 or above
on deck, high	1.56	1.40	1.27	1.19	1.11	1.05	1.00
on deck, low	1.42	1.30	1.21	1.14	1.09	1.04	1.00
'tween-deck	1.26	1.19	1.14	1.09	1.06	1.03	1.00
lower hold	1.15	1.12	1.09	1.06	1.04	1.02	1.00

The following cautions should be observed:

> In the case of marked roll resonance with amplitudes above ±30°, the given figures of transverse acceleration may be exceeded. Effective measures should be taken to avoid this condition.

In the case of heading into the seas at high speed with marked slamming shocks, the given figures of longitudinal and vertical acceleration may be exceeded. An appropriate reduction of speed should be considered.

In the case of running before large stern or quartering seas with a stability which does not amply exceed the accepted minimum requirements, large roll amplitudes must be expected with transverse accelerations greater than the figures given. An appropriate change of heading should be considered.

Forces by wind and sea to cargo units above the weather deck should be accounted for by a simple approach:

force by wind pressure $= 1$ kN per m^2

force by sea sloshing $= 1$ kN per m^2

Sloshing by sea can induce forces much greater than the figure given above. This figure should be considered as remaining unavoidable after adequate measures to prevent overcoming seas.

Sea sloshing forces need only be applied to a height of deck cargo up to 2 m above the weather deck or hatch top.

For voyages in a restricted area, sea sloshing forces may be neglected.

7.2 Balance of forces and moments

The balance calculation should preferably be carried out for:

- transverse sliding in port and starboard directions;

- transverse tipping in port and starboard directions;

- longitudinal sliding under conditions of reduced friction in forward and aft directions.

In the case of symmetrical securing arrangements, one appropriate calculation is sufficient.

Friction contributes towards prevention of sliding. The following friction coefficients (μ) should be applied.

Table 5 – *Friction coefficients*

Materials in contact	Friction coefficient (μ)
Timber–timber, wet or dry	0.4
Steel–timber or steel–rubber	0.3
Steel–steel, dry	0.1
Steel–steel, wet	0.0

7.2.1 Transverse sliding

The balance calculation should meet the following condition (see also figure 17):

$$F_y \leq \mu \cdot m \cdot g + CS_1 \cdot f_1 + CS_2 \cdot f_2 + \ldots + CS_n \cdot f_n$$

where

n is the number of lashings being calculated

F_y is transverse force from load assumption (kN)

μ is friction coefficient

m is mass of the cargo unit (t)

g is gravity acceleration of earth = 9.81 m/s^2

CS is calculated strength of transverse securing devices (kN)

$$CS = \frac{MSL}{1.5}$$

f is a function of μ and the vertical securing angle α (see table 6).

A vertical securing angle α greater than 60° will reduce the effectiveness of this particular securing device in respect to sliding of the unit. Disregarding of such devices from the balance of forces should be considered, unless the necessary load is gained by the imminent tendency to tipping or by a reliable pre-tensioning of the securing device and maintaining the pre-tension throughout the voyage.

Any horizontal securing angle, i.e., deviation from the transverse direction, should not exceed 30°, otherwise an exclusion of this securing device from the transverse sliding balance should be considered.

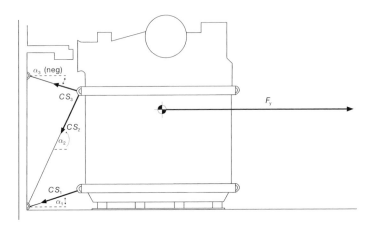

Figure 17 – *Balance of transverse forces*

Table 6 – f *values as a function of* α *and* μ

α \ μ	$-30°$	$-20°$	$-10°$	$0°$	$10°$	$20°$	$30°$	$40°$	$50°$	$60°$	$70°$	$80°$	$90°$
0.3	0.72	0.84	0.93	1.00	1.04	1.04	1.02	0.96	0.87	0.76	0.62	0.47	0.30
0.1	0.82	0.91	0.97	1.00	1.00	0.97	0.92	0.83	0.72	0.59	0.44	0.27	0.10
0.0	0.87	0.94	0.98	1.00	0.98	0.94	0.87	0.77	0.64	0.50	0.34	0.17	0.00

Remark: $f = \mu \cdot \sin \alpha + \cos \alpha$

As an alternative to using table 6 to determine the forces in a securing arrangement, the method outlined in paragraph 7.3 can be used to take account of transverse and longitudinal components of lashing forces.

7.2.2 Transverse tipping

This balance calculation should meet the following condition (see also figure 18):

$$F_y \cdot a \leq b \cdot m \cdot g + CS_1 \cdot c_1 + CS_2 \cdot c_2 + \ldots + CS_n \cdot c_n$$

where

    F_y, m, g, CS, n are as explained under 7.2.1

    a is lever-arm of tipping (m) (see figure 18)

    b is lever-arm of stableness (m) (see figure 18)

    c is lever-arm of securing force (m) (see figure 18)

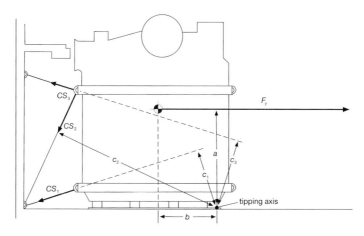

Figure 18 – *Balance of transverse moments*

7.2.3 Longitudinal sliding

Under normal conditions the transverse securing devices provide sufficient longitudinal components to prevent longitudinal sliding. If in doubt, a balance calculation should meet the following condition:

$$F_x \leq \mu \cdot (m \cdot g - F_z) + CS_1 \cdot f_1 + CS_2 \cdot f_2 + \ldots + CS_n \cdot f_n$$

where

F_x is longitudinal force from load assumption (kN)

μ, m, g, f, n are as explained under 7.2.1

F_z is vertical force from load assumption (kN)

CS is calculated strength of longitudinal securing devices (kN)

$$CS = \frac{MSL}{1.5}$$

Remark: Longitudinal components of transverse securing devices should not be assumed greater than $0.5 \cdot CS$.

7.2.4 Calculated example

A calculated example for this method is shown in appendix 1 of annex 13.

7.3 Balance of forces – alternative method

The balance of forces described in paragraph 7.2.1 and 7.2.3 will normally furnish a sufficiently accurate determination of the adequacy of the securing arrangement. However, this alternative method allows a more precise consideration of horizontal securing angles.

Securing devices usually do not have a pure longitudinal or transverse direction in practice but have an angle β in the horizontal plane. This horizontal securing angle β is defined in this annex as the angle of deviation from the transverse direction. The angle β is to be scaled in the quadrantal mode, i.e., between 0° and 90°.

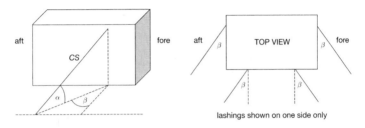

Figure 19 – *Definition of the vertical and horizontal securing angles α and β*

A securing device with an angle β develops securing effects both in longitudinal and transverse direction, which can be expressed by multiplying the calculated strength CS with the appropriate values of f_x or f_y. The values of f_x and f_y can be obtained from table 7.

Table 7 consists of five sets of figures, one each for the friction coefficients μ = 0.4, 0.3, 0.2, 0.1 and 0. Each set of figures is obtained by using the vertical angle α and horizontal angle β. The value of f_x is obtained when entering the table with β from the right while f_y is obtained when entering with β from the left, using the nearest tabular value for α and β. Interpolation is not required but may be used.

The balance calculations are made in accordance with the following formulae:

Transverse sliding: $F_y \le \mu \cdot m \cdot g + f_{y1} \cdot CS_1 + \ldots + f_{yn} \cdot CS_n$

Longitudinal sliding: $F_x \le \mu \cdot (m \cdot g - F_z) + f_{x1} \cdot CS_1 + \ldots + f_{xn} \cdot CS_n$

Transverse tipping: $F_y \cdot a \le b \cdot m \cdot g + 0.9 \cdot (CS_1 \cdot c_1 + CS_2 \cdot c_2 + \ldots + CS_n \cdot c_n)$

Caution:

Securing devices which have a vertical angle α of less than 45° in combination with horizontal angle β greater than 45° should not be used in the balance of transverse tipping in the above formula.

All symbols used in these formulae have the same meaning as defined in paragraph 7.2 except f_y and f_x, obtained from table 7, and CS is as follows:

$$CS = \frac{MSL}{1.35}$$

A calculated example for this method is shown in appendix 1 of annex 13.

Table 7 – f_x *values and* f_y *values as a function of* α, β *and* μ

Table 7.1 for $\mu = 0.4$

β for f_y	α														β for f_x
	–30	**–20**	**–10**	**0**	**10**	**20**	**30**	**40**	**45**	**50**	**60**	**70**	**80**	**90**	
0	0.67	0.80	0.92	1.00	1.05	1.08	1.07	1.02	0.99	0.95	0.85	0.72	0.57	0.40	**90**
10	0.65	0.79	0.90	0.98	1.04	1.06	1.05	1.01	0.98	0.94	0.84	0.71	0.56	0.40	**80**
20	0.61	0.75	0.86	0.94	0.99	1.02	1.01	0.98	0.95	0.91	0.82	0.70	0.56	0.40	**70**
30	0.55	0.68	0.78	0.87	0.92	0.95	0.95	0.92	0.90	0.86	0.78	0.67	0.54	0.40	**60**
40	0.46	0.58	0.68	0.77	0.82	0.86	0.86	0.84	0.82	0.80	0.73	0.64	0.53	0.40	**50**
50	0.36	0.47	0.56	0.64	0.70	0.74	0.76	0.75	0.74	0.72	0.67	0.60	0.51	0.40	**40**
60	0.23	0.33	0.42	0.50	0.56	0.61	0.63	0.64	0.64	0.63	0.60	0.55	0.48	0.40	**30**
70	0.10	0.18	0.27	0.34	0.41	0.46	0.50	0.52	0.52	0.53	0.52	0.49	0.45	0.40	**20**
80	–0.05	0.03	0.10	0.17	0.24	0.30	0.35	0.39	0.41	0.42	0.43	0.44	0.42	0.40	**10**
90	–0.20	–0.14	–0.07	0.00	0.07	0.14	0.20	0.26	0.28	0.31	0.35	0.38	0.39	0.40	**0**

Table 7.2 for $\mu = 0.3$

β for f_y	α														β for f_x
	–30	**–20**	**–10**	**0**	**10**	**20**	**30**	**40**	**45**	**50**	**60**	**70**	**80**	**90**	
0	0.72	0.84	0.93	1.00	1.04	1.04	1.02	0.96	0.92	0.87	0.76	0.62	0.47	0.30	**90**
10	0.70	0.82	0.92	0.98	1.02	1.03	1.00	0.95	0.91	0.86	0.75	0.62	0.47	0.30	**80**
20	0.66	0.78	0.87	0.94	0.98	0.99	0.96	0.91	0.88	0.83	0.73	0.60	0.46	0.30	**70**
30	0.60	0.71	0.80	0.87	0.90	0.92	0.90	0.86	0.82	0.79	0.69	0.58	0.45	0.30	**60**
40	0.51	0.62	0.70	0.77	0.81	0.82	0.81	0.78	0.75	0.72	0.64	0.54	0.43	0.30	**50**
50	0.41	0.50	0.58	0.64	0.69	0.71	0.71	0.69	0.67	0.64	0.58	0.50	0.41	0.30	**40**
60	0.28	0.37	0.44	0.50	0.54	0.57	0.58	0.58	0.57	0.55	0.51	0.45	0.38	0.30	**30**
70	0.15	0.22	0.28	0.34	0.39	0.42	0.45	0.45	0.45	0.45	0.43	0.40	0.35	0.30	**20**
80	0.00	0.06	0.12	0.17	0.22	0.27	0.30	0.33	0.33	0.34	0.35	0.34	0.33	0.30	**10**
90	–0.15	–0.10	–0.05	0.00	0.05	0.10	0.15	0.19	0.21	0.23	0.26	0.28	0.30	0.30	**0**

Table 7.3 for $\mu = 0.2$

β for f_y	α														β for f_x
	–30	**–20**	**–10**	**0**	**10**	**20**	**30**	**40**	**45**	**50**	**60**	**70**	**80**	**90**	
0	0.77	0.87	0.95	1.00	1.02	1.01	0.97	0.89	0.85	0.80	0.67	0.53	0.37	0.20	**90**
10	0.75	0.86	0.94	0.98	1.00	0.99	0.95	0.88	0.84	0.79	0.67	0.52	0.37	0.20	**80**
20	0.71	0.81	0.89	0.94	0.96	0.95	0.91	0.85	0.81	0.76	0.64	0.51	0.36	0.20	**70**
30	0.65	0.75	0.82	0.87	0.89	0.88	0.85	0.79	0.75	0.71	0.61	0.48	0.35	0.20	**60**
40	0.56	0.65	0.72	0.77	0.79	0.79	0.76	0.72	0.68	0.65	0.56	0.45	0.33	0.20	**50**
50	0.46	0.54	0.60	0.64	0.67	0.67	0.66	0.62	0.60	0.57	0.49	0.41	0.31	0.20	**40**
60	0.33	0.40	0.46	0.50	0.53	0.54	0.53	0.51	0.49	0.47	0.42	0.36	0.28	0.20	**30**
70	0.20	0.25	0.30	0.34	0.37	0.39	0.40	0.39	0.38	0.37	0.34	0.30	0.26	0.20	**20**
80	0.05	0.09	0.14	0.17	0.21	0.23	0.25	0.26	0.26	0.26	0.26	0.25	0.23	0.20	**10**
90	–0.10	–0.07	–0.03	0.00	0.03	0.07	0.10	0.13	0.14	0.15	0.17	0.19	0.20	0.20	**0**

Table 7.4 for $\mu = 0.1$

β for f_y	α														β for f_x
	−30	**−20**	**−10**	**0**	**10**	**20**	**30**	**40**	**45**	**50**	**60**	**70**	**80**	**90**	
0	0.82	0.91	0.97	1.00	1.00	0.97	0.92	0.83	0.78	0.72	0.59	0.44	0.27	0.10	**90**
10	0.80	0.89	0.95	0.98	0.99	0.96	0.90	0.82	0.77	0.71	0.58	0.43	0.27	0.10	**80**
20	0.76	0.85	0.91	0.94	0.94	0.92	0.86	0.78	0.74	0.68	0.56	0.42	0.26	0.10	**70**
30	0.70	0.78	0.84	0.87	0.87	0.85	0.80	0.73	0.68	0.63	0.52	0.39	0.25	0.10	**60**
40	0.61	0.69	0.74	0.77	0.77	0.75	0.71	0.65	0.61	0.57	0.47	0.36	0.23	0.10	**50**
50	0.51	0.57	0.62	0.64	0.65	0.64	0.61	0.56	0.53	0.49	0.41	0.31	0.21	0.10	**40**
60	0.38	0.44	0.48	0.50	0.51	0.50	0.48	0.45	0.42	0.40	0.34	0.26	0.19	0.10	**30**
70	0.25	0.29	0.32	0.34	0.35	0.36	0.35	0.33	0.31	0.30	0.26	0.21	0.16	0.10	**20**
80	0.10	0.13	0.15	0.17	0.19	0.20	0.20	0.20	0.19	0.19	0.17	0.15	0.13	0.10	**10**
90	−0.05	−0.03	−0.02	0.00	0.02	0.03	0.05	0.06	0.07	0.08	0.09	0.09	0.10	0.10	**0**

Table 7.5 for $\mu = 0.0$

β for f_y	α														β for f_x
	−30	**−20**	**−10**	**0**	**10**	**20**	**30**	**40**	**45**	**50**	**60**	**70**	**80**	**90**	
0	0.87	0.94	0.98	1.00	0.98	0.94	0.87	0.77	0.71	0.64	0.50	0.34	0.17	0.00	**90**
10	0.85	0.93	0.97	0.98	0.97	0.93	0.85	0.75	0.70	0.63	0.49	0.34	0.17	0.00	**80**
20	0.81	0.88	0.93	0.94	0.93	0.88	0.81	0.72	0.66	0.60	0.47	0.32	0.16	0.00	**70**
30	0.75	0.81	0.85	0.87	0.85	0.81	0.75	0.66	0.61	0.56	0.43	0.30	0.15	0.00	**60**
40	0.66	0.72	0.75	0.77	0.75	0.72	0.66	0.59	0.54	0.49	0.38	0.26	0.13	0.00	**50**
50	0.56	0.60	0.63	0.64	0.63	0.60	0.56	0.49	0.45	0.41	0.32	0.22	0.11	0.00	**40**
60	0.43	0.47	0.49	0.50	0.49	0.47	0.43	0.38	0.35	0.32	0.25	0.17	0.09	0.00	**30**
70	0.30	0.32	0.34	0.34	0.34	0.32	0.30	0.26	0.24	0.22	0.17	0.12	0.06	0.00	**20**
80	0.15	0.16	0.17	0.17	0.17	0.16	0.15	0.13	0.12	0.11	0.09	0.06	0.03	0.00	**10**
90	0.00	0.00	0.00	0.00	0.00	0.00	0.00	0.00	0.00	0.00	0.00	0.00	0.00	0.00	**0**

Remark: $f_y = \cos \alpha \cdot \cos \beta + \mu \cdot \sin \alpha$ $\quad$ $f_x = \cos \alpha \cdot \sin \beta + \mu \cdot \sin \alpha$.

Appendix 1 of annex 13

Calculated example 1

(refer to paragraph 7.2, Balance of forces and moments)

Ship: $L = 120$ m; $B = 20$ m; $GM = 1.4$ m; speed = 15 knots

Cargo: $m = 62$ t; dimensions = $6 \times 4 \times 4$ m;
stowage at $0.7L$ on deck, low

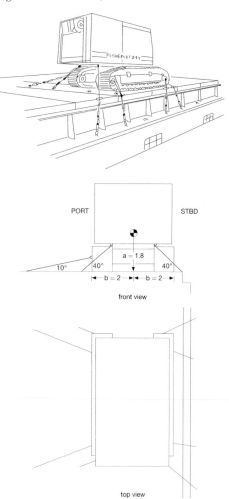

front view

top view

Securing material:

      wire rope: . . . .   breaking strength = 125 kN;
                                             MSL = 100 kN

      shackles, turnbuckles, deck rings: breaking strength = 180 kN;
                                             MSL = 90 kN

      stowage on dunnage boards: . . . . . . μ = 0.3; CS = 90/1.5 = 60 kN

Securing arrangement:

side	n	CS	α	f	c
STBD	4	60 kN	40°	0.96	–
PORT	2	60 kN	40°	0.96	–
PORT	2	60 kN	10°	1.04	–

External forces:

$F_x = 2.9 \times 0.89 \times 62 + 16 + 8 = 184$ kN

$F_y = 6.3 \times 0.89 \times 62 + 24 + 12 = 384$ kN

$F_z = 6.2 \times 0.89 \times 62 = 342$ kN

Balance of forces (STBD arrangement):

$384 < 0.3 \times 62 \times 9.81 + 4 \times 60 \times 0.96$

$384 < 412$ this is OK!

Balance of forces (PORT arrangement):

$384 < 0.3 \times 62 \times 9.81 + 2 \times 60 \times 0.96 + 2 \times 60 \times 1.04$

$384 < 422$ this is OK!

Balance of moments:

$384 \times 1.8 < 2 \times 62 \times 9.81$

$691 < 1216$ no tipping, even without lashings!

Calculated example 2

(refer to paragraph 7.3, Balance of forces – alternative method)

A cargo unit of 68 t mass is stowed on timber ($\mu = 0.3$) in the 'tween deck at 0.7L of a vessel. $L = 160$ m, $B = 24$ m, $v = 18$ kN and GM $= 1.5$ m. Dimensions of the cargo unit are height $= 2.4$ m and width $= 1.8$ m. The external forces are: $F_x = 112$ kN, $F_y = 312$ kN, $F_z = 346$ kN.

The top view shows the overall securing arrangement with eight lashings.

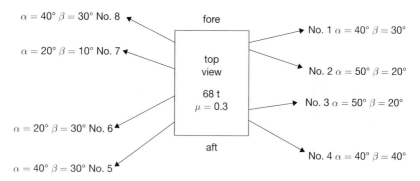

Calculation of balance of forces:

No.	MSL (kN)	CS (kN)	α	β	f_y	CS × f_y	f_x	CS × f_x
1	108	80	40° stbd	30° fwd	0.86	68.8 stbd	0.58	46.4 fwd
2	90	67	50° stbd	20° aft	0.83	55.6 stbd	0.45	30.2 aft
3	90	67	50° stbd	20° fwd	0.83	55.6 stbd	0.45	30.2 fwd
4	108	80	40° stbd	40° aft	0.78	62.4 stbd	0.69	55.2 aft
5	108	80	40° port	30° aft	0.86	68.8 port	0.58	46.4 aft
6	90	67	20° port	30° aft	0.92	61.6 port	0.57	38.2 aft
7	90	67	20° port	10° fwd	1.03	69.0 port	0.27	18.1 fwd
8	108	80	40° port	30° fwd	0.86	68.8 port	0.58	46.4 fwd

Transverse balance of forces (STBD arrangement) Nos. 1, 2, 3 and 4:

$$312 < 0.3 \times 68 \times 9.81 + 68.8 + 55.6 + 55.6 + 62.4$$

$$312 < 443 \text{ this is OK!}$$

Transverse balance of forces (PORT arrangement) Nos. 5, 6, 7 and 8:

$$312 < 0.3 \times 68 \times 9.81 + 68.8 + 61.6 + 69.0 + 68.8$$
$$312 < 468 \text{ this is OK!}$$

Longitudinal balance of forces (FWD arrangement) Nos. 1, 3, 7, 8:

$$112 < 0.3 \, (68 \times 9.81 - 346) + 46.4 + 30.2 + 18.1 + 46.4$$
$$112 < 237 \text{ this is OK!}$$

Longitudinal balance of forces (AFT arrangement) Nos. 2, 4, 5, 6:

$$112 < 0.3 \, (68 \times 9.81 - 346) + 30.2 + 55.2 + 46.4 + 38.2$$
$$112 < 266 \text{ this is OK!}$$

Transverse tipping

Unless specific information is provided, the vertical centre of gravity of the cargo unit can be assumed to be at one half the height and the transverse centre of gravity at one half the width. Also, if the lashing is connected as shown in the sketch, instead of measuring c, the length of the lever from the tipping axis to the lashing CS, it is conservative to assume that it is equal to the width of the cargo unit.

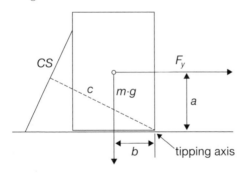

$$F_y . a \qquad \le b \cdot m \cdot g + 0.9 \cdot (CS_1 \cdot c_1 + CS_2 \cdot c_2 + CS_3 \cdot c_3 + CS_4 \cdot c_4)$$
$$312 \times 2.4/2 \; < 1.8/2 \times 68 \times 9.81 + 0.9 \times 1.8 \times (80 + 67 + 67 + 80)$$
$$374 \qquad\qquad < 600 + 476$$
$$374 \qquad\qquad < 1076 \text{ this is OK!}$$

Appendix 2 of annex 13

Explanations and interpretation of "Methods to assess the efficiency of securing arrangements for non-standardized cargo"

1   The exclusion of very heavy units as carried under the provisions of paragraph 1.8 of chapter 1 of the Code from the scope of application of the methods should be understood to accommodate the possibility of adapting the stowage and securing of such units to specifically determined weather conditions and sea conditions during transport. The exclusion should not be understood as being a restriction of the methods to units up to a certain mass or dimension.

2   The acceleration figures given in table 2, in combination with the correction factors, represent peak values on a 25-day voyage. This does not imply that peak values in x, y and z directions occur simultaneously with the same probability. It can be generally assumed that peak values in the transverse direction will appear in combination with less than 60% of the peak values in longitudinal and vertical directions.

Peak values in longitudinal and vertical directions may be associated more closely because they have the common source of pitching and heaving.

3   The advanced calculation method uses the "worst case approach". That is expressed clearly by the transverse acceleration figures, which increase to forward and aft in the ship and thereby show the influence of transverse components of simultaneous vertical accelerations. Consequently there is no need to consider vertical accelerations separately in the balances of transverse forces and moments. These simultaneously acting vertical accelerations create an apparent increase of weight of the unit and thus increase the effect of the friction in the balance of forces and the moment of stableness in the balance of moments. For this reason there is no reduction of the force $m \cdot g$ normal to the deck due to the presence of an angle of heel.

The situation is different for the longitudinal sliding balance. The worst case would be a peak value of the longitudinal force F_x accompanied by an extreme reduction of weight through the vertical force F_z.

4   The friction coefficients shown in the methods are somewhat reduced against appropriate figures in other publications. The reason for this should be seen in various influences which may appear in practical shipping, as: moisture, grease, oil, dust and other residues, vibration of the ship.

There are certain stowage materials available which are said to increase friction considerably. Extended experience with these materials may bring additional coefficients into practical use.

5   The principal way of calculating forces within the securing elements of a complex securing arrangement should necessarily include the consideration of:

– load–elongation behaviour (elasticity),

– geometrical arrangement (angles, length),

– pre-tension

of each individual securing element.

This approach would require a large volume of information and a complex, iterative calculation. The results would still be doubtful due to uncertain parameters.

Therefore the simplified approach was chosen with the assumption that the elements take an even load of CS (calculated strength) which is reduced against the MSL (maximum securing load) by the safety factor.

6   When employing the advanced calculation method, the way of collecting data should be followed as shown in the calculated example. It is acceptable to estimate securing angles, to take average angles for a set of lashings and similarly to arrive at reasonable figures of the levers *a*, *b* and *c* for the balance of moments.

It should be borne in mind that meeting or missing the balance calculation just by a tiny change of one or the other parameters indicates to be near the limit anyway. There is no clear-cut borderline between safety and non-safety. If in doubt, the arrangement should be improved.

Note on annex 14

Member Governments are invited to bring the amendments to the CSS Code (annex 14) to the attention of shipowners, ship operators, shipmasters and crews and all other parties concerned and, in particular, encourage shipowners and terminal operators to:

.1 apply the amendments in their entirety for containerships, the keels of which were laid or which are at a similar stage of construction **on or after 1 January 2015**;

.2 apply sections 4.4, 7.1, 7.3 and 8 to existing containerships, the keels of which were laid or which are at a similar stage of construction **before 1 January 2015**; and

.3 apply the principles of this guidance contained in sections 6 and 7.2 **to existing containerships** as far as practical by the flag State Administration with the understanding that existing ships would not be required to be enlarged or undergo other major structural modifications as determined.

Annex 14

Guidance on providing safe working conditions for securing of containers on deck

1 Aim

To ensure that persons engaged in carrying out container securing operations on deck have safe working conditions and, in particular safe access, appropriate securing equipment and safe places of work. These guidelines should be taken into account at the design stage when securing systems are devised. These guidelines provide shipowners, ship builders, classification societies, Administrations and ship designers with guidance on producing or authorizing a Cargo Safe Access Plan (CSAP).

2 Scope

Ships which are specifically designed and fitted for the purpose of carrying containers on deck.

3 Definitions

3.1 *Administration* means the Government of the State whose flag the ship is entitled to fly.

3.2 *Fencing* is a generic term for guardrails, safety rails, safety barriers and similar structures that provide protection against the falls of persons.

3.3 *Lashing positions* include positions:

.1 in between container stows on hatch covers;

.2 at the end of hatches;

.3 on outboard lashing stanchions/pedestals;

.4 outboard lashing positions on hatch covers; and

.5 any other position where people work with container securing.

3.4 *SATLs* are semi-automatic twistlocks.

3.5 *Securing* includes lashing and unlashing.

3.6   *Stringers* are the uprights or sides of a ladder.

3.7   *Turnbuckles and lashing rods*[*] include similar cargo securing devices.

4   General

4.1   Introduction

4.1.1   Injuries to dockworkers on board visiting ships account for the majority of accidents that occur within container ports, with the most common activity that involves such injuries being the lashing/unlashing of deck containers. Ships' crew engaged in securing operations face similar dangers.

4.1.2   During the design and construction of containerships the provision of a safe place of work for lashing personnel is essential.

4.1.3   Containership owners and designers are reminded of the dangers associated with container securing operations and urged to develop and use container securing systems which are safe by design. The aim should be to eliminate or at least minimize the need for:

   .1   container top work;

   .2   work in other equally hazardous locations; and

   .3   the use of heavy and difficult to handle securing equipment.

4.1.4   It should be borne in mind that providing safe working conditions for securing containers deals with matters relating to design, operation, and maintenance, and that the problems on large containerships are not the same as on smaller ones.

4.2   Revised Recommendations on safety of personnel during container securing operations (MSC.1/Circ.1263)

Shipowners, ship designers and Administrations should take into account the recommendations on safe design of securing arrangements contained in these guidelines, and in the Recommendations on safety of personnel during container securing operations (MSC.1/Circ.1263).

4.3   Cargo Safe Access Plan (CSAP)

4.3.1 The Guidelines for the preparation of the Cargo Securing Manual (MSC/Circ.745) requires ships which are specifically designed and fitted for

---

[*] Refer to standard ISO 3874, Annex D Lashing rod systems and tensioning devices.

the purpose of carrying containers to have an approved Cargo Safe Access Plan (CSAP) on board, for all areas where containers are secured.

4.3.2 Stakeholders, including, but not limited to shipowners, ship designers, ship builders, Administrations, classification societies and lashing equipment manufacturers, should be involved at an early stage in the design of securing arrangements on containerships and in the development of the CSAP.

4.3.3 The CSAP should be developed at the design stage in accordance with chapter 5 of the annex to MSC.1/Circ.1353.

4.3.4 Designers should incorporate the recommendations of this annex into the CSAP so that safe working conditions can be maintained during all anticipated configurations of container stowage.

4.4   Training and familiarization

4.4.1 Personnel engaged in cargo securing operations should be trained in the lashing and unlashing of containers as necessary to carry out their duties in a safe manner. This should include the different types of lashing equipment that are expected to be used.

4.4.2 Personnel engaged in cargo securing operations should be trained in the identification and handling of bad order or defective securing gear in accordance with each ship's procedures to ensure damaged gear is segregated for repair and maintenance or disposal.

4.4.3 Personnel engaged in cargo securing operations should be trained to develop the knowledge and mental and physical manual handling skills that they require to do their job safely and efficiently, and to develop general safety awareness to recognize and avoid potential dangers.

4.4.4 Personnel should be trained in safe systems of work. Where personnel are involved in working at heights, they should be trained in the use of relevant equipment. Where practical, the use of fall protection equipment should take precedence over fall arrest systems.

4.4.5 Personnel who are required to handle thermal cables and/or connect and disconnect temperature control units should be given training in recognizing defective cables, receptacles and plugs.

4.4.6 Personnel engaged in containership cargo operations should be familiarized with the ship's unique characteristics and potential hazards arising from such operations necessary to carry out their duties.

5 Responsibilities of involved parties

5.1 Administrations should ensure that:

.1 lashing plans contained within the approved Cargo Securing Manual are compatible with the current design of the ship and the intended container securing method is both safe and physically possible;

.2 the Cargo Securing Manual, lashing plans and the CSAP are kept up to date; and

.3 lashing plans and the CSAP are compatible with the design of the vessel and the equipment available.

5.2 Shipowners and operators should ensure that:

.1 portable cargo securing devices are certified and assigned with a maximum securing load (MSL). The MSL should be documented in the cargo securing manual as required by the CSS Code;

.2 the operational recommendations of this annex are complied with;

.3 correction, changes or amendments of the Cargo Securing Manual, lashing plans and the Cargo Safe Access Plan (CSAP) should be promptly sent to the competent authority for approval; and

.4 only compatible and certified equipment in safe condition is used.

5.3 Designers should follow design recommendations of these guidelines.

5.4 Shipbuilders should follow design recommendations of these guidelines.

5.5 Containership terminal operators should ensure that the recommendations of relevant parts of this annex are complied with.

6 Design

6.1 General design considerations

6.1.1 *Risk assessment*

6.1.1.1 Risk assessments should be performed at the design stage taking into account the recommendations of this annex to ensure that securing operations can be safely carried out in all anticipated container configurations. This assessment should be conducted with a view toward developing the Cargo Safe Access Plan (CSAP). Hazards to be assessed should include but not be limited to:

.1　slips, trips and falls;

.2　falls from height;

.3　injuries whilst manually handling lashing gear;

.4　being struck by falling lashing gear or other objects;

.5　potential damage due to container operations. High-risk areas should be identified in order to develop appropriate protection or other methods of preventing significant damage;

.6　adjacent electrical risks (temperature controlled unit cable connections, etc.);

.7　the adequacy of the access to all areas that is necessary to safely perform container securing operations;

.8　ergonomics (e.g., size and weight of equipment) of handling lashing equipment; and

.9　implications of lashing 9′6″ high, or higher, containers and mixed stows of 40′ and 45′ containers.

6.1.1.2　Shipbuilders should collaborate with designers of securing equipment in conducting risk assessments and ensure that the following basic criteria are adhered to when building containerships.

6.1.2　Ship designers should ensure that container securing operations performed in outer positions can be accomplished safely. As a minimum, a platform should be provided on which to work safely. This platform should have fencing to prevent workers falling off it.

6.1.3　The space provided between the container stows for workers to carry out lashing operations should provide:

.1　a firm and level working surface;

.2　a working area, excluding lashings in place, to provide a clear sight of twist lock handles and allow for the manipulation of lashing gear;

.3　sufficient spaces to permit the lashing gear and other equipment to be stowed without causing a tripping hazard;

.4   sufficient spaces between the fixing points of the lashing bars on deck, or on the hatch covers, to tighten the turnbuckles;

.5   access in the form of ladders on hatch coamings;

.6   safe access to lashing platforms;

.7   protective fencing on lashing platforms; and

.8   adequate lighting in line with these guidelines.

6.1.4   Ship designers should aim to eliminate the need to access and work on the tops of deck stows.

6.1.5   Platforms should be designed to provide a clear work area, unencumbered by deck piping and other obstructions and take into consideration:

.1   containers must be capable of being stowed within safe reach of the workers using the platform; and

.2   the work area size and the size of the securing components used.

6.2   Provisions for safe access

6.2.1   General provisions

6.2.1.1   The minimum clearance for transit areas should be at least 2 m high and 600 mm wide.

6.2.1.2   All relevant deck surfaces used for movement about the ship and all passageways and stairs should have non-slip surfaces.

6.2.1.3   Where necessary for safety, walkways on deck should be delineated by painted lines or otherwise marked by pictorial signs.

6.2.1.4   All protrusions in access ways, such as cleats, ribs and brackets that may give rise to a trip hazard should be highlighted in a contrasting colour.

6.2.2   Lashing position design (platforms, bridges and other lashing positions)

6.2.2.1   Lashing positions should be designed to eliminate the use of three high lashing bars and be positioned in close proximity to lashing equipment stowage areas. Lashing positions should be designed to provide a clear work area which is unencumbered by deck piping and other obstructions and take into consideration:

.1   the need for containers to be stowed within safe reach of the personnel using the lashing position so that the horizontal operating distance from the securing point to the container does not exceed 1,100 mm and not less than 220 mm for lashing bridges and 130 mm for other positions;

.2   the size of the working area and the movement of lashing personnel; and

.3   the length and weight of lashing gear and securing components used.

6.2.2.2 The width of the lashing positions should preferably be 1,000 mm, but not less than 750 mm.

6.2.2.3 The width of permanent lashing bridges should be:

.1   750 mm between top rails of fencing; and

.2   a clear minimum of 600 mm between storage racks, lashing cleats and any other obstruction.

6.2.2.4 Platforms on the end of hatches and outboard lashing stations should preferably be at the same level as the top of the hatch covers.

6.2.2.5 Toe boards (or kick plates) should be provided around the sides of elevated lashing bridges and platforms to prevent securing equipment from falling and injuring people. Toe boards should preferably be 150 mm high; however, where this is not possible they should be at least 100 mm high.

6.2.2.6 Any openings in the lashing positions through which people can fall should be possible to be closed.

6.2.2.7 Lashing positions should not contain obstructions, such as storage bins or guides to reposition hatch covers.

6.2.2.8 Lashing positions which contain removable sections should be capable of being temporarily secured.

6.2.3   *Fencing design*

6.2.3.1 Bridges and platforms, where appropriate, should be fenced. As a minimum, fencing design should take into consideration:

.1   the strength and height of the rails should be designed to prevent workers from falling;

> **.2** flexibility in positioning the fencing of gaps. A horizontal unfenced gap should not be greater than 300 mm;
>
> **.3** provisions for locking and removal of fencing as operational situations change based on stowage anticipated for that area;
>
> **.4** damage to fencing and how to prevent failure due to that damage; and
>
> **.5** adequate strength of any temporary fittings. These should be capable of being safely and securely installed.

6.2.3.2 The top rail of fencing should be 1 m high from the base, with two intermediate rails. The opening below the lowest course of the guard rails should not exceed 230 mm. The other courses should be not more than 380 mm apart.

6.2.3.3 Where possible fences and handrails should be highlighted with a contrasting colour to the background.

6.2.3.4 Athwartships cargo securing walkways should be protected by adequate fencing if an unguarded edge exists when the hatch cover is removed.

6.2.4   Ladder and manhole design

6.2.4.1 Where a fixed ladder gives access to the outside of a lashing position, the stringers should be connected at their extremities to the guardrails of the lashing position, irrespective of whether the ladder is sloping or vertical.

6.2.4.2 Where a fixed ladder gives access to a lashing position through an opening in the platform, the opening shall be protected with either a fixed grate with a lock back mechanism, which can be closed after access, or fencing. Grabrails should be provided to ensure safe access through the opening.

6.2.4.3 Where a fixed ladder gives access to a lashing position from the outside of the platform, the stringers of the ladder should be opened above the platform level to give a clear width of 700 to 750 mm to enable a person to pass through the stringers.

6.2.4.4 A fixed ladder should not slope at an angle greater than 25° from the vertical. Where the slope of a ladder exceeds 15° from the vertical, the ladder should be provided with suitable handrails not less than 540 mm apart, measured horizontally.

6.2.4.5 A fixed vertical ladder of a height exceeding 3 m, and any fixed vertical ladder, from which a person may fall into a hold, should be fitted with guard hoops, which should be constructed in accordance with paragraphs 6.2.4.6 and 6.2.4.7.

6.2.4.6 The ladder hoops should be uniformly spaced at intervals not exceeding 900 mm and should have a clearance of 750 mm from the rung to the back of the hoop and be connected by longitudinal strips secured to the inside of the hoops, each equally spaced round the circumference of the hoop.

6.2.4.7 The stringers should be carried above the floor level of the platform by at least 1 m and the ends of the stringers should be given lateral support and the top step or rung should be level with the floor of the platform unless the steps or rungs are fitted to the ends of the stringers.

6.2.4.8 As far as practicable, access ladders and walkways, and work platforms should be designed so that workers do not have to climb over piping or work in areas with permanent obstructions.

6.2.4.9 There should be no unprotected openings in any part of the workplace. Access opening must be protected with handrails or access covers that can be locked back during access.

6.2.4.10 As far as practicable, manholes should not be situated in transit areas; however, if they are, proper fencing should protect them.

6.2.4.11 Access ladders and manholes should be large enough for persons to safely enter and leave.

6.2.4.12 A foothold at least 150 mm deep should be provided.

6.2.4.13 Handholds should be provided at the top of the ladder to enable safe access to the platform to be gained.

6.2.4.14 Manhole openings that may present a fall hazard should be highlighted in contrasting colour around the rim of the opening.

6.2.4.15 Manhole openings at different levels of the lashing bridge should not be located directly below one another, as far as practicable.

6.3 Lashing systems

6.3.1 *General provisions*

Lashing systems, including tensioning devices, should:

.1 conform to international standards,[*] where applicable;

---

[*] Refer to standard ISO 3874 – The Handling and Securing of Type 1 Freight Containers, annex A-D.

.2 be compatible with the planned container stowages;

.3 be compatible with the physical ability of persons to safely hold, deploy and use such equipment;

.4 be uniform and compatible, e.g., twistlocks and lashing rod heads should not interfere with each other;

.5 be subject to a periodic inspection and maintenance regime. Non-conforming items should be segregated for repair or disposal; and

.6 be according to the CSM.

6.3.2 Twistlock design

6.3.2.1 Shipowners should ensure that the number of different types of twistlocks provided for cargo securing is kept to a minimum and clear instructions are provided for their operation. The use of too many different types of twistlocks may lead to confusion as to whether the twistlocks are locked.

6.3.2.2 The design of twistlocks should ensure the following:

.1 positive locking with easy up and down side identification;

.2 dislodging from corner fitting is not possible even when grazing a surface;

.3 access and visibility of the unlocking device is effective in operational situations;

.4 unlocked positions are easily identifiable and do not relock inadvertently due to jolting or vibration; and

.5 unlocking poles are as light as possible, of a simple design for ease of use.

6.3.2.3 Where it is not feasible to entirely eliminate working on the tops of container stows, the twistlock designs used should minimize the need for such working, e.g., use of SATLs, fully automatic twistlocks or similar design.

6.3.3 Lashing rod design

6.3.3.1 The design of containership securing systems should take into account the practical abilities of the workers to lift, reach, hold, control and connect the components called for in all situations anticipated in the cargo securing plan.

6.3.3.2 The maximum length of a lashing rod should be sufficient to reach the bottom corner fitting of a container on top of two high cube containers and be used in accordance with the instructions provided by the manufacturers.

6.3.3.3 The weight of lashing rods should be minimized as low as possible consistent with the necessary mechanical strength.

6.3.3.4 The head of the lashing rod that is inserted in the corner fitting should be designed with a pivot/hinge or other appropriate device so that the rod does not come out of the corner fitting accidentally.

6.3.3.5 The rod's length in conjunction with the length and design of the turnbuckle should be such that the need of extensions is eliminated when lashing high cube (9′6″) containers.

6.3.3.6 Lightweight rods should be provided where special tools are needed to lash high cube containers.

6.3.4 *Turnbuckle design*

6.3.4.1 Turnbuckle end fittings should be designed to harmonize with the design of lashing rods.

6.3.4.2 Turnbuckles should be designed to minimize the work in operating them.

6.3.4.3 Anchor points for turnbuckles should be positioned to provide safe handling and to prevent the bending of rods.

6.3.4.4 To prevent hand injury during tightening or loosening motions, there should be a minimum distance of 70 mm between turnbuckles.

6.3.4.5 The turnbuckle should incorporate a locking mechanism which will ensure that the lashing does not work loose during the voyage.

6.3.4.6 The weight of turnbuckles should be minimized as low as possible consistent with the necessary mechanical strength.

6.3.5 *Storage bins and lashing equipment stowage design*

6.3.5.1 Bins or stowage places for lashing materials should be provided.

6.3.5.2 All lashing gear should be stowed as close to its intended place of use as possible.

6.3.5.3 The stowage of securing devices should be arranged so they can easily be retrieved from their stowage location.

6.3.5.4 Bins for faulty or damaged gear should also be provided and appropriately marked.

6.3.5.5 Bins should be of sufficient strength.

6.3.5.6 Bins and their carriers should be designed to be lifted off the vessel and restowed.

6.4 Lighting design

A lighting plan should be developed to provide for:

.1 the proper illumination of access ways, not less than 10 lux (1 foot candle),* taking into account the shadows created by containers that may be stowed in the area to be lit, for example different length containers in or over the work area;

.2 a separate fixed or temporary (where necessary) lighting system for each working space between the container bays, which is bright enough, not less than 50 lux (5 foot candle),* for the work to be done, but minimizes glare to the deck workers;

.3 such illumination should, where possible, be designed as a permanent installation and adequately guarded against breakage; and

.4 the illumination intensity should take into consideration the distance to the uppermost reaches where cargo securing equipment is utilized.

7 Operational and maintenance procedures

7.1 Introduction

7.1.1 Procedures for safe lashing and securing operations should be included in the ship's Safety Management System as part of the ISM Code documentation.

---

* Refer to Safety and Health in Ports, ILO Code of Practice, section 7.1.5.

7.1.2 Upon arrival of the ship, a safety assessment of the lashing positions and the access to those positions should be made before securing work commences.

7.2 Operational procedures

7.2.1 Container deck working

7.2.1.1 Transit areas should be safe and clear of cargo and all equipment.

7.2.1.2 Openings that are necessary for the operation of the ship, which are not protected by fencing, should be closed during cargo securing work. Any necessarily unprotected openings in work platforms (i.e., those with a potential fall of less than 2 m), and gaps and apertures on deck should be properly highlighted.

7.2.1.3 The use of fencing is essential to prevent falls. When openings in safety barriers are necessary to allow container crane movements, particularly with derricking cranes, removable fencing should be used whenever possible.

7.2.1.4 It should be taken into account that when lifting lashing bars that can weigh between 11 and 21 kg and turnbuckles between 16 and 23 kg, there may be a risk of injury and severe illness as a result of physical strain if handled above shoulder height with the arms extended. It is therefore recommended that personnel work in pairs to reduce the individual workload in securing the lashing gear.

7.2.1.5 The company involved with cargo operation should anticipate, identify, evaluate and control hazards and take appropriate measures to eliminate or minimize potential hazards to prevent in particular harmful lumbar spinal damage and severe illness as a result of physical strain.

7.2.1.6 Personnel engaged in containership cargo operations should wear appropriate Personnel Protective Equipment (PPE) whilst carrying out lashing operations. The PPE should be provided by the company.

7.2.1.7 Manual twistlocks should only be used where safe access is provided.

7.2.1.8 Containers should not be stowed in spaces configured for larger sized containers unless they can be secured under safe working conditions.

7.2.2   Container top working

7.2.2.1   When work on container tops can not be avoided, safe means of access should be provided by the container cargo operation terminal, unless the ship has appropriate means of access in accordance with the CSAP.

7.2.2.2   Recommended practice involves the use of a safety cage lifted by a spreader to minimize the risk to personnel.

7.2.2.3   A safe method of work should be developed and implemented to ensure the safety of lashers when on the top of container stows on deck. Where practical, the use of fall prevention equipment should take precedence over fall arrest equipment.

7.2.3   *Failure to provide safe lashing stations on board/carry out lashing by port workers*

7.2.3.1   Where there are lashing and unlashing locations on board ship where no fall protection, such as adequate handrails are provided, and no other safe method can be found, the containers should not be lashed or unlashed and the situation should be reported to shoreside supervisor and the master or deck officer immediately.

7.2.3.2   If protective systems cannot be designed to provide safe protected access and lashing work positions, in all cargo configurations then cargo should not be stowed in that location. Neither crew nor shore workers should be subjected to hazardous working conditions in the normal course of securing cargo.

7.3   Maintenance

7.3.1   In line with section 2.3 (Inspection and maintenance schemes) of the Revised guidelines for the preparation of the Cargo Securing Manual (MSC.1/Circ.1353) all ships should maintain a record book, which should contain the procedures for accepting, maintaining and repairing or rejecting of cargo securing devices. The record book should also contain a record of inspections.

7.3.2   Lighting should be properly maintained.

7.3.3   Walkways, ladders, stairways and fencings should be subject to a periodic maintenance programme which will reduce/prevent corrosion and prevent subsequent collapse.

7.3.4 Corroded walkways, ladders, stairways and fencings should be repaired or replaced as soon as practicable. The repairs should be effected immediately if the corrosion could prevent safe operations.

7.3.5 It should be borne in mind that turnbuckles covered with grease are difficult to handle when tightening.

7.3.6 Storage bins and their carriers should be maintained in a safe condition.

8 Specialized container safety design

8.1 Temperature controlled unit power outlets should provide a safe, watertight electrical connection.

8.2 Temperature controlled unit power outlets should feature a heavy duty, interlocked and circuit breaker protected electrical power outlet. This should ensure the outlet can not be switched "live" until a plug is fully engaged and the actuator rod is pushed to the "On" position. Pulling the actuator rod to the "Off" position should manually de-energize the circuit.

8.3 The temperature controlled unit power circuit should de-energize automatically if the plug is accidentally withdrawn while in the "On" position. Also, the interlock mechanism should break the circuit while the pin and sleeve contacts are still engaged. This provides total operator safety and protection against shock hazard while eliminating arcing damage to the plug and receptacle.

8.4 Temperature controlled unit power outlets should be designed to ensure that the worker is not standing directly in front of the socket when switching takes place.

8.5 The positioning of the temperature controlled unit feed outlets should not be such that the flexible cabling needs to be laid out in such a way as to cause a tripping hazard.

8.6 Stevedores or ship's crew who are required to handle temperature controlled unit cables and/or connect and disconnect reefer units should be given training in recognizing defective wires and plugs.

8.7 Means or provisions should be provided to lay the temperature controlled unit cables in and protect them from lashing equipment falling on them during lashing operations.

8.8   Defective or inoperative temperature controlled unit plugs/electrical banks should be identified and confirmed as "locked out/tagged out" by the vessel.

9   References

ILO Code of Practice – *Safety and Health in Ports*

ILO Convention 152 – *Occupational Safety and Health in Dock Work*

ISO Standard 3874 – *The Handling and Securing of Type 1 Freight Containers*

International Convention on Load Lines, 1966, as modified by the 1988 LL Protocol

Revised Recommendation on safety of personnel during container securing operations (MSC.1/Circ.1263)

Revised guidelines for the preparation of the Cargo Securing Manual (MSC.1/Circ.1353).

Appendices

Appendix 1

Resolution A.489(XII)
adopted 19 November 1981

Safe stowage and securing of cargo units and other entities in ships other than cellular containerships

THE ASSEMBLY,

RECALLING Article 16(i) of the Convention on the Inter-Governmental Maritime Consultative Organization,*

RECOGNIZING that there is a need to improve standards of stowage and securing of cargo units and other entities in ships other than cellular containerships,

RECOGNIZING ALSO that special attention should be paid to the stowage of cargo in cargo units and on vehicles,

BELIEVING that the universal application of improved standards would be greatly facilitated if all cargo units, vehicles and other entities for shipment were provided with means for applying portable securing gear,

CONSIDERING that a universal improvement in the standards could best be achieved on an international basis,

1.　ADOPTS the Guidelines on the Safe Stowage and Securing of Cargo Units and Other Entities in Ships Other Than Cellular Containerships, the text of which is annexed to the present resolution;

2.　RECOMMENDS Governments to issue guidelines for the safe stowage and securing of cargo units and other entities in ships other than cellular containerships in conformity with the annexed Guidelines and, in particular, to require such ships entitled to fly the flag of their State to carry a Cargo Securing Manual as described in the annexed Guidelines.

---

* The name of the Organization was changed to "International Maritime Organization" (IMO) by virtue of amendments to its Convention adopted on 22 May 1982.

Annex

Guidelines on the safe stowage and securing of cargo units and other entities in ships other than cellular containerships

1   *Cargo units and other entities* in this context means wheeled cargo, containers, flats, pallets, portable tanks, packaged units, vehicles, etc., and parts of loading equipment which belong to the ship and which are not fixed to the ship.

2   These guidelines apply to the securing of cargo units or other entities on open or closed decks of ships other than cellular containerships and ships specially designed and fitted for the purpose of carrying containers. Application of the guidelines should always be at the master's discretion.

3   Applicable parts of the International Maritime Dangerous Goods Code and resolution A.288(VIII) on stowage and securing of containers on deck in ships which are not specially designed and fitted for the purpose of carrying containers should be observed.

4   Shippers' special advice or guidelines regarding handling and stowage of individual cargo units should be observed.

5   When reasonable, cargo units and other entities should be provided with means for safe application of portable securing gear. Such means should be of sufficient strength to withstand the forces which may be encountered on board ships in a seaway.

6   Cargo units and other entities should be stowed in a safe manner and secured as necessary to prevent tipping and sliding. Due regard should be paid to the forces and accelerations to which the cargo units and other entities may be subjected.

7   Ships should be provided with fixed cargo securing arrangements and with portable securing gear. Information regarding technical properties and practical application of the various items of securing equipment on board should be provided.

8   Administrations should ascertain that every ship to which these guidelines apply is provided with a Cargo Securing Manual appropriate to the characteristics of the ship and its intended service, in particular the ship's main dimensions, its hydrostatic properties, the weather and sea conditions which may be expected in the ship's trading area and also the cargo composition.

9   Where there is reason to suspect that cargo within any unit is packed or stowed in an unsatisfactory way, or that a vehicle is in a bad state of repair, or where the unit itself cannot be safely stowed and secured on the ship, and may therefore be a source of danger to ship or crew, such unit or vehicle should not be accepted for shipment.

Cargo Securing Manual

10   The information contained in the Cargo Securing Manual should include the following items as appropriate:

.1   details of fixed securing arrangements and their locations (padeye, eyebolts, elephant-feet, etc.);

.2   locations and stowage of portable securing gear;

.3   details of portable securing gear including an inventory of items provided and their strengths;

.4   examples of correct application of portable securing gear on various cargo units, vehicles and other entities carried on the ship;

.5   indication of the variation of transverse, longitudinal and vertical accelerations to be expected in various positions on board the ship.

Appendix 2

Revised guidelines for the preparation of the Cargo Securing Manual

MSC.1/Circ.1353

1   In accordance with regulations VI/5 and VII/5 of the 1974 SOLAS Convention, as amended, cargo units and cargo transport units shall be loaded, stowed and secured throughout the voyage in accordance with the Cargo Securing Manual approved by the Administration, which shall be drawn up to a standard at least equivalent to the guidelines developed by the Organization.

2   The Maritime Safety Committee, at its eighty-seventh session (12 to 21 May 2010), considered the proposal by the Sub-Committee on Dangerous Goods, Solid Cargoes and Containers, at its fourteenth session (21 to 25 September 2009), and approved the revised guidelines for the preparation of the Cargo Securing Manual, as set out in the annex.

3   These revised guidelines are based on the provisions contained in the annex to MSC/Circ.745 but have been expanded to include the safe access for lashing of containers, taking into account the provisions of the Code of Safe Practice for Cargo Stowage and Securing (CSS Code), as amended. They are of a general nature and intended to provide guidance on the preparation of such Cargo Securing Manuals, which are required on all types of ships engaged in the carriage of cargoes other than solid and liquid bulk cargoes.

4   Member Governments are invited to bring these guidelines to the attention of all parties concerned, with the aim of having Cargo Securing Manuals carried on board ships prepared appropriately and in a consistent manner, and to:

.1   apply the revised guidelines in their entirety for containerships, the keels of which were laid or which are at a similar stage of construction on or after 1 January 2015; and

.2   apply chapters 1 to 4 of the revised guidelines to existing containerships, the keels of which were laid or which were at a similar stage of construction before 1 January 2015.

5   This circular supersedes MSC/Circ.745.

Annex

*Revised guidelines for the preparation of the Cargo Securing Manual**

Preamble

1   In accordance with the International Convention for the Safety of Life at Sea, 1974 (SOLAS) chapters VI, VII and the Code of Safe Practice for Cargo Stowage and Securing (CSS Code), cargo units, including containers shall be stowed and secured throughout the voyage in accordance with a Cargo Securing Manual, approved by the Administration.

2   The Cargo Securing Manual is required on all types of ships engaged in the carriage of all cargoes other than solid and liquid bulk cargoes.

3   The purpose of these guidelines is to ensure that Cargo Securing Manuals cover all relevant aspects of cargo stowage and securing and to provide a uniform approach to the preparation of Cargo Securing Manuals, their layout and content. Administrations may continue accepting Cargo Securing Manuals drafted in accordance with Containers and cargoes (BC) – Cargo Securing Manual (MSC/Circ.385) provided that they satisfy the requirements of these guidelines.

4   If necessary, those manuals should be revised explicitly when the ship is intended to carry containers in a standardized system.

5   It is important that securing devices meet acceptable functional and strength criteria applicable to the ship and its cargo. It is also important that the officers on board are aware of the magnitude and direction of the forces involved and the correct application and limitations of the cargo securing devices. The crew and other persons employed for the securing of cargoes should be instructed in the correct application and use of the cargo securing devices on board the ship.

---

* Apply the revised guidelines in their entirety for containerships, the keels of which were laid or which are at a similar stage of construction on or after 1 January 2015.

Chapter 1 – General[*]

1.1 Definitions

1.1.1 *Cargo securing devices* are all fixed and portable devices used to secure and support cargo units.

1.1.2 *Maximum securing load (MSL)* is a term used to define the allowable load capacity for a device used to secure cargo to a ship. *Safe working load (SWL)* may be substituted for MSL for securing purposes, provided this is equal to or exceeds the strength defined by MSL.

1.1.3 *Standardized cargo* means cargo for which the ship is provided with an approved securing system based upon cargo units of specific types.

1.1.4 *Semi-standardized cargo* means cargo for which the ship is provided with a securing system capable of accommodating a limited variety of cargo units, such as vehicles, trailers, etc.

1.1.5 *Non-standardized cargo* means cargo which requires individual stowage and securing arrangements.

1.2 Preparation of the Manual

The Cargo Securing Manual should be developed, taking into account the recommendations given in these guidelines, and should be written in the working language or languages of the ship. If the language or languages used is not English, French or Spanish, a translation into one of these languages should be included.

1.3 General information

This chapter should contain the following general statements:

.1 "The guidance given herein should by no means rule out the principles of good seamanship, neither can it replace experience in stowage and securing practice."

---

[*] Apply chapters 1 to 4 of the revised guidelines to existing containerships, the keels of which were laid or which were at a similar stage of construction before 1 January 2015.

.2 "The information and requirements set forth in this Manual are consistent with the requirements of the vessel's trim and stability booklet, International Load Line Certificate (1966), the hull strength loading manual (if provided) and with the requirements of the International Maritime Dangerous Goods (IMDG) Code (if applicable)."

.3 "This Cargo Securing Manual specifies arrangements and cargo securing devices provided on board the ship for the correct application to and the securing of cargo units, containers, vehicles and other entities, based on transverse, longitudinal and vertical forces which may arise during adverse weather and sea conditions."

.4 "It is imperative to the safety of the ship and the protection of the cargo and personnel that the securing of the cargo is carried out properly and that only appropriate securing points or fittings should be used for cargo securing."

.5 "The cargo securing devices mentioned in this manual should be applied so as to be suitable and adapted to the quantity, type of packaging, and physical properties of the cargo to be carried. When new or alternative types of cargo securing devices are introduced, the Cargo Securing Manual should be revised accordingly. Alternative cargo securing devices introduced should not have less strength than the devices being replaced."

.6 "There should be a sufficient quantity of reserve cargo securing devices on board the ship."

.7 "Information on the strength and instructions for the use and maintenance of each specific type of cargo securing device, where applicable, is provided in this manual. The cargo securing devices should be maintained in a satisfactory condition. Items worn or damaged to such an extent that their quality is impaired should be replaced."

.8 The Cargo Safe Access Plan (CSAP) is intended to provide detailed information for persons engaged in work connected with cargo stowage and securing. Safe access should be provided and maintained in accordance with this plan.

Chapter 2 – Securing devices and arrangements

2.1   Specification for fixed cargo securing devices

This sub-chapter should indicate and where necessary illustrate the number, locations, type and MSL of the fixed devices used to secure cargo and should as a minimum contain the following information:

2.1.1   a list and/or plan of the fixed cargo securing devices, which should be supplemented with appropriate documentation for each type of device as far as practicable. The appropriate documentation should include information as applicable regarding:

> **.1**   name of manufacturer;
>
> **.2**   type designation of item with simple sketch for ease of identification;
>
> **.3**   material(s);
>
> **.4**   identification marking;
>
> **.5**   strength test result or ultimate tensile strength test result;
>
> **.6**   result of non destructive testing; and
>
> **.7**   Maximum Securing Load (MSL);

2.1.2   fixed securing devices on bulkheads, web frames, stanchions, etc. and their types (e.g., pad eyes, eyebolts, etc.), where provided, including their MSL;

2.1.3   fixed securing devices on decks and their types (e.g., elephant feet fittings, container fittings, apertures, etc.) where provided, including their MSL;

2.1.4   fixed securing devices on deckheads, where provided, listing their types and MSL; and

2.1.5   for existing ships with non-standardized fixed securing devices, the information on MSL and location of securing points is deemed sufficient.

2.2   Specification for portable cargo securing devices

This sub-chapter should describe the number of and the functional and design characteristics of the portable cargo securing devices carried on board the ship, and should be supplemented by suitable drawings or sketches if deemed necessary. It should contain the following information as applicable:

2.2.1 a list for the portable securing devices, which should be supplemented with appropriate documentation for each type of device, as far as practicable. The appropriate documentation should include information as applicable regarding:

.1 name of manufacturer;

.2 type designation of item with simple sketch for ease of identification;

.3 material(s), including minimum safe operational temperature;

.4 identification marking;

.5 strength test result or ultimate tensile strength test result;

.6 result of non destructive testing; and

.7 Maximum Securing Load (MSL);

2.2.2 container stacking fittings, container deck securing fittings, fittings for interlocking of containers, bridge-fittings, etc., their MSL and use;

2.2.3 chains, wire lashings, rods, etc., their MSL and use;

2.2.4 tensioners (e.g., turnbuckles, chain tensioners, etc.), their MSL and use;

2.2.5 securing gear for cars, if appropriate, and other vehicles, their MSL and use;

2.2.6 trestles and jacks, etc., for vehicles (trailers) where provided, including their MSL and use; and

2.2.7 anti-skid material (e.g., soft boards) for use with cargo units having low frictional characteristics.

2.3   Inspection and maintenance schemes

This sub-chapter should describe inspection and maintenance schemes of the cargo securing devices on board the ship.

2.3.1 Regular inspections and maintenance should be carried out under the responsibility of the master. Cargo securing devices inspections as a minimum should include:

.1 routine visual examinations of components being utilized; and

.2 periodic examinations/re-testing as required by the Administration. When required, the cargo securing devices concerned should be subjected to inspections by the Administration.

2.3.2 This sub-chapter should document actions to inspect and maintain the ship's cargo securing devices. Entries should be made in a record book, which should be kept with the Cargo Securing Manual. This record book should contain the following information:

.1 procedures for accepting, maintaining and repairing or rejecting cargo securing devices; and

.2 record of inspections.

2.3.3 This sub-chapter should contain information for the master regarding inspections and adjustment of securing arrangements during the voyage.

2.3.4 Computerized maintenance procedures may be referred to in this sub-chapter.

Chapter 3 – Stowage and securing of non-standardized and semi-standardized cargo

3.1 Handling and safety instructions

This sub-chapter should contain:

.1 instructions on the proper handling of the securing devices; and

.2 safety instructions related to handling of securing devices and to securing and unsecuring of units by ship or shore personnel.

3.2 Evaluation of forces acting on cargo units

This sub-chapter should contain the following information:

.1 tables or diagrams giving a broad outline of the accelerations which can be expected in various positions on board the ship in adverse sea conditions and with a range of applicable metacentric height (GM) values;

.2 examples of the forces acting on typical cargo units when subjected to the accelerations referred to in paragraph 3.2.1 and angles of roll and metacentric height (GM) values above which the forces acting on the cargo units exceed the permissible limit for the specified securing arrangements as far as practicable;

> **.3** examples of how to calculate number and strength of portable securing devices required to counteract the forces referred to in 3.2.2 as well as safety factors to be used for different types of portable cargo securing devices. Calculations may be carried out according to Annex 13 to the CSS Code or methods accepted by the Administration;
>
> **.4** it is recommended that the designer of a Cargo Securing Manual converts the calculation method used into a form suiting the particular ship, its securing devices and the cargo carried. This form may consist of applicable diagrams, tables or calculated examples; and
>
> **.5** other operational arrangements such as electronic data processing (EDP) or use of a loading computer may be accepted as alternatives to the requirements of the above paragraphs 3.2.1 to 3.2.4, providing that this system contains the same information.

3.3 Application of portable securing devices on various cargo units, vehicles and stowage blocks

3.3.1 This sub-chapter should draw the master's attention to the correct application of portable securing devices, taking into account the following factors:

> **.1** duration of the voyage;
>
> **.2** geographical area of the voyage with particular regard to the minimum safe operational temperature of the portable securing devices;
>
> **.3** sea conditions which may be expected;
>
> **.4** dimensions, design and characteristics of the ship;
>
> **.5** expected static and dynamic forces during the voyage;
>
> **.6** type and packaging of cargo units including vehicles;
>
> **.7** intended stowage pattern of the cargo units including vehicles; and
>
> **.8** mass and dimensions of the cargo units and vehicles.

3.3.2 This sub-chapter should describe the application of portable cargo securing devices as to number of lashings and allowable lashing angles. Where necessary, the text should be supplemented by suitable drawings or sketches to facilitate the correct understanding and proper application of the securing devices to various types of cargo and cargo units. It should be pointed out that for certain cargo units and other entities with low friction resistance, it is advisable to place soft boards or other anti-skid material under the cargo to increase friction between the deck and the cargo.

3.3.3   This sub-chapter should contain guidance as to the recommended location and method of stowing and securing of containers, trailers and other cargo carrying vehicles, palletized cargoes, unit loads and single cargo items (e.g., woodpulp, paper rolls, etc.), heavy weight cargoes, cars and other vehicles.

3.4   Supplementary requirements for ro–ro ships

3.4.1   The manual should contain sketches showing the layout of the fixed securing devices with identification of strength (MSL) as well as longitudinal and transverse distances between securing points. In preparing this sub-chapter further guidance should be utilized from IMO Assembly resolutions A.533(13) and A.581(14), as amended, as appropriate.

3.4.2   In designing securing arrangements for cargo units, including vehicles and containers, on ro–ro passenger ships and specifying minimum strength requirements for securing devices used, forces due to the motion of the ship, angle of heel after damage or flooding and other considerations relevant to the effectiveness of the cargo securing arrangement should be taken into account.

3.5   Bulk carriers

If bulk carriers carry cargo units falling within the scope of chapter VI/5 or chapter VII/5 of the SOLAS Convention, this cargo shall be stowed and secured in accordance with a Cargo Securing Manual, approved by the Administration.

Chapter 4 – Stowage and securing of containers and other standardized cargo

4.1   Handling and safety instructions

This sub-chapter should contain:

.1   instructions on the proper handling of the securing devices; and

.2 safety instructions related to handling of securing devices and to securing and unsecuring of containers or other standardized cargo by ship or shore personnel.

4.2 Stowage and securing instructions

This sub-chapter is applicable to any stowage and securing system (i.e., stowage within or without cellguides) for containers and other standardized cargo. On existing ships the relevant documents regarding safe stowage and securing may be integrated into the material used for the preparation of this chapter.

4.2.1 Stowage and securing plan

This sub-chapter should consist of a comprehensive and understandable plan or set of plans providing the necessary overview on:

.1 longitudinal and athwartship views of under deck and on deck stowage locations of containers as appropriate;

.2 alternative stowage patterns for containers of different dimensions;

.3 maximum stack masses;

.4 permissible vertical sequences of masses in stacks;

.5 maximum stack heights with respect to approved sight lines; and

.6 application of securing devices using suitable symbols with due regard to stowage position, stack mass, sequence of masses in stack and stack height. The symbols used should be consistent throughout the Cargo Securing Manual.

4.2.2 Stowage and securing principle on deck and under deck

This sub-chapter should support the interpretation of the stowage and securing plan with regard to container stowage, highlighting:

.1 the use of the specified devices; and

.2 any guiding or limiting parameters as dimension of containers, maximum stack masses, sequence of masses in stacks, stacks affected by wind load, height of stacks.

It should contain specific warnings of possible consequences from misuse of securing devices or misinterpretation of instructions given.

4.3   Other allowable stowage patterns

4.3.1   This sub-chapter should provide the necessary information for the master to deal with cargo stowage situations deviating from the general instructions addressed under sub-chapter 4.2, including appropriate warnings of possible consequences from misuse of securing devices or misinterpretation of instructions given.

4.3.2   Information should be provided with regard to, *inter alia*:

.1   alternative vertical sequences of masses in stacks;

.2   stacks affected by wind load in the absence of outer stacks;

.3   alternative stowage of containers with various dimensions; and

.4   permissible reduction of securing effort with regard to lower stack masses, lesser stack heights or other reasons.

4.4   Forces acting on cargo units

4.4.1   This sub-chapter should present the distribution of accelerations on which the stowage and securing system is based, and specify the underlying condition of stability. Information on forces induced by wind and sea on deck cargo should be provided.

4.4.2   It should further contain information on the nominal increase of forces or accelerations with an increase of initial stability. Recommendations should be given for reducing the risk of cargo losses from deck stowage by restrictions to stack masses or stack heights, where high initial stability cannot be avoided.

Chapter 5 – Cargo safe access plan (CSAP)

5.1   Ships which are specifically designed and fitted for the purpose of carrying containers should be provided with a Cargo Safe Access Plan (CSAP) in order to demonstrate that personnel will have safe access for container securing operations. This plan should detail arrangements necessary for the conducting of cargo stowage and securing in a safe manner.

It should include the following for all areas to be worked by personnel:

.1   hand rails;

.2   platforms;

.3   walkways;

.4 ladders;

.5 access covers;

.6 location of equipment storage facilities;

.7 lighting fixtures;

.8 container alignment on hatch covers/pedestals;

.9 fittings for specialized containers, such as reefer plugs/ receptacles;

.10 first aid stations and emergency access/egress;

.11 gangways; and

.12 any other arrangements necessary for the provision of safe access.

5.2   Guidelines for specific requirements are contained in annex 14 to the CSS Code.

Appendix 3

Resolution A.533(13)
adopted 17 November 1983
as amended by MSC.1/Circ.1354

Elements to be taken into account when considering the safe stowage and securing of cargo units and vehicles in ships

THE ASSEMBLY,

RECALLING Article 16(j) of the Convention on the International Maritime Organization concerning the functions of the Assembly in relation to regulations concerning maritime safety,

RECALLING FURTHER that at its twelfth session it adopted resolution A.489(XII) regarding safe stowage and securing of cargo units and other entities in ships other than cellular containerships,

TAKING ACCOUNT of the IMO/ILO guidelines for training in the packing of cargo in freight containers,

RECOGNIZING that cargo units and vehicles are transported in increasing numbers on seagoing ships,

RECOGNIZING FURTHER that the cargo is stowed on and secured to cargo units and vehicles in most cases at the shipper's premises or at inland terminals and transported by road or rail to ports prior to the seagoing voyage and that the cargo on cargo units and vehicles may not always be adequately stowed or secured for safe sea transport,

REALIZING that adequately stowed and secured cargoes on cargo units and vehicles for road and rail transport in most cases would also be capable of withstanding the forces imposed on them during the sea leg of the transport,

ACKNOWLEDGING that there is a need for cargo units and vehicles presented for transport by sea to be fitted with satisfactory securing arrangements for securing them to the ship, arrangements for the securing of the cargo within the cargo unit or vehicle to facilitate its safe stowage and securing therein and for ships to be fitted with adequate securing points,

BELIEVING that the universal application of improved standards and securing arrangements is best facilitated if the elements to be taken into account when considering such matters are known to, and considered by, all links in the transport chain,

BELIEVING FURTHER that this can best be achieved on an international basis,

HAVING CONSIDERED the recommendation made by the Maritime Safety Committee at its forty-eighth session,

1.   INVITES Governments to issue recommendations to the different links in the transport chain in their countries, responsible for the transport of cargo units and vehicles intended for, and including, sea transport, taking into account the elements set out in the annex to this resolution,

2.   REQUESTS the Secretary-General to bring these elements to the attention of Member Governments and international organizations responsible for the safety of road, rail and sea transport in order that they can be taken into account in the design and construction of cargo units and vehicles and the design and construction of the ships in which they are carried.

Annex

Elements to be taken into account when considering the safe stowage and securing of cargo units and vehicles in ships*

The elements which should be taken into account relate specifically to the safe shipment of cargo units, including vehicles. The aim is to indicate to the various parties involved the principal factors and features which need to be considered when designing and operating the ship or presenting the cargo unit, or vehicle, for such shipment. In addition, it is hoped that the elements will facilitate and promote better understanding of the problems and the needs of the masters of ships so engaged.

1   The parties involved

1.1   The elements are intended primarily for the information and guidance of the following parties which, it is considered, are in some way associated

---

* *Cargo units* in this context means wheeled or tracked cargo, containers, flats, portable tanks, vehicles and the ship's mobile cargo handling equipment not fixed to the ship.

with either the design or the operation of the ship or, alternatively, with the design, presentation or loading of cargo units including vehicles. They are:

.1 shipbuilders;

.2 shipowners;

.3 shipmasters;

.4 port authorities;

.5 shippers;

.6 forwarding agents;

.7 road hauliers;

.8 stevedores;

.9 cargo unit and vehicle manufacturers;

.10 insurers;

.11 railway operators; and

.12 packers of containers at inland depots.

2   General elements

2.1   It is of the utmost importance to ensure that:

.1 cargo units including vehicles intended for the carriage of cargo in sea transport are in sound structural condition and have an adequate number of securing points of sufficient strength so that they can be satisfactorily secured to the ship. Vehicles should, in addition, be provided with an effective braking system;

.2 cargo units and vehicles are provided with an adequate number of securing points to enable the cargo to be adequately secured to the cargo unit or vehicle so as to withstand the forces, in particular the transverse forces, which may arise during the sea transport; and

.3 safe access and safe places of work are provided for persons engaged in work connected with cargo stowage and securing.

3   Elements to be considered by the shipowner and shipbuilder

3.1   The ship should be provided with an adequate number of securing points of sufficient strength, a sufficient number of items of cargo securing gear of sufficient strength and a Cargo Securing Manual. In considering the number and strength of the securing points, items of cargo securing gear and the preparation of the Cargo Securing Manual, the following elements should be taken into account:

.1 duration of the voyage;

.2 geographical area of the voyage;

.3 sea conditions which may be expected;

.4 size, design and characteristics of the ship;

.5 dynamic forces under adverse weather conditions;

.6 types of cargo units and vehicles to be carried;

.7 intended stowage pattern of the cargo units and vehicles;

.8 weight of cargo units and vehicles; and

.9 safe access, safe place of work, illumination and working conditions for persons engaged in work connected with cargo stowage and securing.

3.2 The Cargo Securing Manual should provide information on the characteristics of cargo securing items and their correct application.

3.3 Ship's mobile cargo handling equipment not fixed to the ship should be provided with adequate securing points.

3.4 Ships which are specifically designed and fitted for the purpose of carrying containers should be provided with a Cargo Safe Access Plan (CSAP) in order to demonstrate that personnel will have safe access for container securing operations.

4 Elements to be considered by the master

4.1 When accepting cargo units or vehicles for shipment and having taken into account the elements listed in paragraph 3.1 above, the master should be satisfied that:

.1 all decks intended for the stowage of cargo units including vehicles are in so far as is practicable free from oil and grease;

.2 cargo units including vehicles are in an apparent good order and condition suitable for sea transport particularly with a view to their being secured;

.3   the ship has on board an adequate supply of cargo securing gear which is maintained in sound working condition;

.4   cargo units including vehicles are adequately stowed on and secured to the cargo unit or vehicle;

.5   where practicable, cargoes are adequately stored on and secured to the cargo unit and vehicle; and

.6   where applicable, safe access to be provided in accordance with the CSAP and maintained throughout cargo operations.

4.2   In addition, cargo spaces should be regularly inspected to ensure that the cargo, cargo units and vehicles remain safely secured throughout the voyage.

5   Elements to be considered by the shipper, forwarding agents, road hauliers and stevedores (and, where appropriate, by the port authorities)

5.1   Shippers or any other party involved with presenting cargo units including vehicles for shipment should appreciate that such items can be subjected to forces of great magnitude, particularly in the transverse direction and especially in adverse weather conditions. Consequently, it is of importance that they should be constantly aware of this fact and that they ensure that:

.1   cargo units including vehicles are suitable for the intended sea transport;

.2   cargo units including vehicles are provided with adequate securing points for the securing of the cargo unit or vehicle to the ship and the cargo to the cargo unit or vehicle;

.3   the cargo in the cargo unit or vehicle is adequately stowed and secured to withstand the forces which may arise during sea transport;

.4   in general the cargo unit or vehicle is clearly marked and provided with documentation to indicate its gross weight and any precautions which may have to be observed during sea transport; and

.5   the CSAP, when applicable, and the lashing plan as required for by the CSM should be provided to the terminal operator in adequate time prior to the arrival of the ships.

Appendix 4

Resolution A.581(14)
adopted 20 November 1985
as amended by MSC/Circ.812 and MSC.1/Circ.1355

Guidelines for securing arrangements for the transport of road vehicles on ro–ro ships

THE ASSEMBLY,

RECALLING Article 15(j) of the Convention on the International Maritime Organization concerning the functions of the Assembly in relation to regulations and guidelines concerning maritime safety,

RECALLING ALSO resolution A.489(XII) on safe stowage and securing of cargo units and other entities in ships other than cellular containerships and MSC/Circ.385[*] of 8 January 1985 containing the provisions to be included in a Cargo Securing Manual to be carried on board ships,

BEARING IN MIND resolution A.533(13) on elements to be taken into account when considering the safe stowage and securing of cargo units and vehicles in ships,

TAKING ACCOUNT of the revised IMO/ILO Guidelines for the Packing of Cargo in Freight Containers and Vehicles,[†]

RECOGNIZING that the marine transport of road vehicles on ro–ro ships is increasing,

RECOGNIZING ALSO that a number of serious accidents have occurred because of inadequate securing arrangements on ships and road vehicles,

RECOGNIZING FURTHER the need for the Organization to establish guidelines for securing arrangements on board ro–ro ships and on road vehicles,

---

[*] MSC/Circ.385 has been revoked by MSC/Circ.745 of 13 June 1996 and further revoked by MSC.1/Circ.1353 of 30 June 2010.

[†] These Guidelines have been replaced by the IMO/ILO/UN ECE Guidelines for packing of cargo transport units.

REALIZING that, given adequately designed ships and properly equipped road vehicles, lashings of sufficient strength will be capable of withstanding the forces imposed on them during the voyage,

REALIZING FURTHER that certain requirements for side guards, particularly those positioned very low on road vehicles, will obstruct the proper securing of the road vehicles on board ro–ro ships and that appropriate measures will have to be taken to satisfy both safety aspects,

BELIEVING that application of the guidelines will enhance safety in the transport of road vehicles on ro–ro ships and that this can be achieved on an international basis,

HAVING CONSIDERED the recommendation made by the Maritime Safety Committee at its fifty-first session,

1.   ADOPTS the Guidelines for Securing Arrangements for the Transport of Road Vehicles on Ro–Ro Ships set out in the annex to the present resolution;

2.   URGES Member Governments to implement these Guidelines at the earliest possible opportunity in respect of new ro–ro ships and new vehicles and, as far as practicable, in respect of existing vehicles which may be transported on ro–ro ships;

3.   REQUESTS the Secretary-General to bring these Guidelines to the attention of Member Governments and relevant international organizations responsible for safety in design and construction of ships and road vehicles for action as appropriate.

Annex

Guidelines for securing arrangements for the transport of road vehicles on ro–ro ships

Preamble

In view of experience in the transport of road vehicles on ro–ro ships, it is recommended that these Guidelines for securing road vehicles on board such ships should be followed. Shipowners and shipyards, when designing and building ro–ro ships to which these Guidelines apply, should take sections 4 and 6 particularly into account. Manufacturers, owners and operators of road vehicles which may be transported on ro–ro ships should take sections 5 and 7 particularly into account.

1   Scope

1.1   These Guidelines for securing and lashing road vehicles on board ro–ro ships outline in particular the securing arrangements on the ship and on the vehicles, and the securing methods to be used.

2   Application

2.1   These Guidelines apply to ro–ro ships which regularly carry road vehicles on either long or short international voyages in unsheltered waters. They concern:

> .1   road vehicles as defined in 3.2.1, 3.2.2, 3.2.3 and 3.2.5 with an authorized maximum total mass of vehicles and cargo of between 3.5 and 40 tonnes; and

> .2   articulated road trains as defined in 3.2.4 with a maximum total mass of not more than 45 tonnes, which can be carried on ro–ro ships.

2.2   These Guidelines do not apply to buses.

2.3   For road vehicles having characteristics outside the general parameters for road vehicles (particularly where the normal height of the centre of gravity is exceeded), the location and the number of securing points should be specially considered.

3   Definitions

3.1   *Ro–ro ship* means a ship which has one or more decks either closed or open, not normally subdivided in any way and generally running the entire length of the ship, in which goods (packaged or in bulk, in or on road vehicles (including road tank-vehicles), trailers, containers, pallets, demountable or portable tanks or in or on similar cargo transport units or other receptacles) can be loaded or unloaded normally in a horizontal direction.

3.2   In these Guidelines the term *road vehicle*[*] includes:

> .1   *Commercial vehicle,* which means a motor vehicle which, on account of its design and appointments, is used mainly for conveying goods. It may also be towing a trailer.

---

[*] Refer to ISO Standard No. 3833.

.2 *Semi-trailer,* which means a trailer which is designed to be coupled to a semi-trailer towing vehicle and to impose a substantial part of its total mass on the towing vehicle.

.3 *Road train,* which means the combination of a motor vehicle with one or more independent trailers connected by a drawbar. (For the purpose of section 5 each element of a road train is considered a separate vehicle.)

.4 *Articulated road train,* which means the combination of a semi-trailer towing vehicle with a semi-trailer.

.5 *Combination of vehicles,* which means a motor vehicle coupled with one or more towed vehicles. (For the purpose of section 5 each element of a combination of vehicles is considered a separate vehicle.)

4 Securing points on ships' decks

4.1 The ship should carry a Cargo Securing Manual in accordance with resolution A.489(XII) containing the information listed and recommended in paragraph 10 of the annex to that resolution.

4.2 The decks of a ship intended for road vehicles as defined in 3.2 should be provided with securing points. The arrangement of securing points should be left to the discretion of the shipowner provided that for each road vehicle or element of a combination of road vehicles, there is the following minimum arrangement of securing points:

.1 The distance between securing points in the longitudinal direction should in general not exceed 2.5 m. However, there may be a need for the securing points in the forward and after parts of the ship to be more closely spaced than they are amidships.

.2 The athwartships spacing of securing points should not be less than 2.8 m nor more than 3 m. However, there may be a need for the securing points in the forward and after parts of the ship to be more closely spaced than they are amidships.

.3 The maximum securing load (MSL) of each securing point should be not less than 100 kN. If the securing point is designed to accommodate more than one lashing (y lashings), the MSL should be not less than $y \times 100$ kN.

4.3 In ro–ro ships which only occasionally carry road vehicles, the spacing and strength of securing points should be such that the special considerations which may be necessary to stow and secure road vehicles safely are taken into account.

5 Securing points on road vehicles

5.1 Securing points on road vehicles should be designed for securing the road vehicles to the ship and should have an aperture capable of accepting only one lashing. The securing point and aperture should permit varying directions of the lashing to the ship's deck.[*]

5.2 The same number of not less than two or not more than six securing points should be provided on each side of the road vehicle in accordance with the provisions of 5.3.

5.3 Subject to the provisions of notes 1, 2 and 3 hereunder, the minimum number and minimum strength of securing points should be in accordance with the following table:

Gross vehicle mass (GVM) (tonnes)	Minimum number of securing points on each side of the road vehicle	Minimum strength without permanent deformation of each securing point as lifted (kN)
$3.5\,t \leq GVM \leq 20\,t$	2	
$20\,t < GVM \leq 30\,t$	3	$\dfrac{GVM \times 10 \times 1.2}{n^*}$
$30\,t < GVM \leq 40\,t$	4	

[*] Where n is the total number of securing points on each side of the road vehicle.

Note 1: For road trains, the table applies to each component, i.e., to the motor vehicle and each trailer, respectively.

Note 2: Semi-trailer towing vehicles are excluded from the table above. They should be provided with two securing points at the front of the vehicle, the strength of which should be sufficient to prevent lateral movement of the front of the vehicle. A towing coupling at the front may replace the two securing points.

Note 3: If the towing coupling is used for securing vehicles other than semi-trailer towing vehicles, this should not replace or be substituted for the above-mentioned minimum number and strength of securing points on each side of the vehicle.

5.4 Each securing point on the vehicle should be marked in a clearly visible colour.

---

[*] If more than one aperture is provided at a securing point, each aperture should have the strength for the securing point in the table in 5.3.

5.5   Securing points on vehicles should be so located as to ensure effective restraint of the vehicle by the lashings.

5.6   Securing points should be capable of transferring the forces from the lashings to the chassis of the road vehicle and should never be fitted to bumpers or axles unless these are specially constructed and the forces are transmitted directly to the chassis.

5.7   Securing points should be so located that lashings can be readily and safely attached, particularly where side-guards are fitted to the vehicle.

5.8   The internal free passage of each securing point's aperture should be not less than 80 mm but the aperture need not be circular in shape.

5.9   Equivalent or superior securing arrangements may be considered for vehicles for which the provisions of table 5.3 are unsuitable.

6   Lashings

6.1   The maximum securing load (MSL) of lashings should not be less than 100 kN and they should be made of material having suitable elongation characteristics. However, for vehicles not exceeding 15 tonnes (GVM), lashings with lower MSL values may be used. The required number and MSL of lashings may be calculated according to annex 13 to the Code of Safe Practice for Cargo Stowage and Securing (CSS Code), taking into consideration the criteria mentioned in paragraph 1.5.1 of the Code.

6.2   Lashings should be so designed and attached that, provided there is safe access, it is possible to tighten them if they become slack. Where practicable and necessary, the lashings should be examined at regular intervals during the voyage and tightened as necessary.

6.3   Lashings should be attached to the securing points with hooks or other devices so designed that they cannot disengage from the aperture of the securing point if the lashing slackens during the voyage.

6.4   Only one lashing should be attached to any one aperture of the securing point on the vehicle.

6.5   Lashings should only be attached to the securing points provided for that purpose.

6.6   Lashings should be attached to the securing points on the vehicle in such a way that the angle between the lashing and the horizontal and vertical planes lies preferably between 30° and 60°.

6.7   Bearing in mind the characteristics of the ship and the weather conditions expected on the intended voyage, the master should decide on the number of securing points and lashings to be used for each voyage.

6.8   Where there is doubt that a road vehicle complies with the provisions of table 5.3, the master may, at his discretion, load the vehicle on board, taking into account the apparent condition of the vehicle, the weather and sea conditions expected on the intended voyage and all other circumstances.

7   Stowage

7.1   Depending on the area of operation, the predominant weather conditions and the characteristics of the ship, road vehicles should be stowed so that the chassis are kept as static as possible by not allowing free play in the suspension of the vehicles. This can be done, for example, by compressing the springs by tightly securing the vehicle to the deck, by jacking up the chassis prior to securing the vehicle or by releasing the air pressure on compressed-air suspension systems.

7.2   Taking into account the conditions referred to in 7.1 and the fact that compressed-air suspension systems may lose air, the air pressure should be released on every vehicle fitted with such a system if the voyage is of more than 24 hours duration. If practicable, the air pressure should be released also on voyages of a shorter duration. If the air pressure is not released, the vehicle should be jacked up to prevent any slackening of the lashings resulting from any air leakage from the system during the voyage.

7.3   Where jacks are used on a vehicle, the chassis should be strengthened in way of the jacking-up points and the position of the jacking-up points should be clearly marked.

7.4   Special consideration should be given to the securing of road vehicles stowed in positions where they may be exposed to additional forces. Where vehicles are stowed athwartship, special consideration should be given to the forces which may arise from such stowage.

7.5   Wheels should be chocked to provide additional security in adverse conditions.

7.6   Vehicles with diesel engines should not be left in gear during the voyage.

7.7   Vehicles designed to transport loads likely to have an adverse effect on their stability, such as hanging meat, should have integrated in their design a means of neutralizing the suspension system.

7.8   Stowage should be arranged in accordance with the following:

   .1   The parking brakes of each vehicle or of each element of a combination of vehicles should be applied and locked.

   .2   Semi-trailers, by the nature of their design, should not be supported on their landing legs during sea transport unless the landing legs are specially designed for that purpose and so marked. An uncoupled semi-trailer should be supported by a trestle or similar device placed in the immediate area of the drawplate so that the connection of the fifth wheel to the kingpin is not restricted. Semi-trailer designers should consider the space and the reinforcements required and the selected areas should be clearly marked.

Appendix 5

Resolution A.864(20)
adopted 27 November 1997

Recommendations for entering enclosed spaces aboard ships

THE ASSEMBLY,

RECALLING Article 15(j) of the Convention on the International Maritime Organization concerning the functions of the Assembly in relation to regulations and guidelines concerning maritime safety,

BEING CONCERNED at the continued loss of life resulting from personnel entering shipboard spaces in which the atmosphere is oxygen-depleted, toxic or flammable,

BEING AWARE of the work undertaken in this regard by the International Labour Organization, Governments and segments of the private sector,

NOTING that the Maritime Safety Committee, at its fifty-ninth session, approved appendix F to the Code of Safe Practice for Solid Bulk Cargoes concerning recommendations for entering cargo spaces, tanks, pump-rooms, fuel tanks, cofferdams, duct keels, ballast tanks and similar enclosed spaces,

NOTING FURTHER the decision of the Maritime Safety Committee at its sixty-sixth session to replace appendix F referred to above with the recommendations annexed to this resolution,

HAVING CONSIDERED the recommendation made by the Maritime Safety Committee at its sixty-sixth session,

1.   ADOPTS the Recommendations for Entering Enclosed Spaces Aboard Ships set out in the annex to the present resolution;

2.   INVITES Governments to bring the annexed Recommendations to the attention of shipowners, ship operators and seafarers, urging them to apply the Recommendations, as appropriate, to all ships;

3.   REQUESTS the Maritime Safety Committee to keep the Recommendations under review and amend them, as necessary.

Annex

Recommendations for entering enclosed spaces aboard ships

Preamble

The object of these recommendations is to encourage the adoption of safety procedures aimed at preventing casualties to ships' personnel entering enclosed spaces where there may be an oxygen-deficient, flammable and/ or toxic atmosphere.

Investigations into the circumstances of casualties that have occurred have shown that accidents on board ships are in most cases caused by an insufficient knowledge of, or disregard for, the need to take precautions rather than a lack of guidance.

The following practical recommendations apply to all types of ships and provide guidance to seafarers. It should be noted that on ships where entry into enclosed spaces may be infrequent, for example, on certain passenger ships or small general cargo ships, the dangers may be less apparent, and accordingly there may be a need for increased vigilance.

The recommendations are intended to complement national laws or regulations, accepted standards or particular procedures which may exist for specific trades, ships or types of shipping operations.

It may be impracticable to apply some recommendations to particular situations. In such cases, every endeavour should be made to observe the intent of the recommendations, and attention should be paid to the risks that may be involved.

1   Introduction

The atmosphere in any enclosed space may be deficient in oxygen and/or contain flammable and/or toxic gases or vapours. Such an unsafe atmosphere could also subsequently occur in a space previously found to be safe. Unsafe atmosphere may also be present in spaces adjacent to those spaces where a hazard is known to be present.

2 Definitions

2.1 *Enclosed space* means a space which has any of the following characteristics:

.1 limited openings for entry and exit;

.2 unfavourable natural ventilation; and

.3 is not designed for continuous worker occupancy,

and includes, but is not limited to, cargo spaces, double bottoms, fuel tanks, ballast tanks, pump-rooms, compressor rooms, cofferdams, void spaces, duct keels, inter-barrier spaces, engine crankcases and sewage tanks.

2.2 *Competent person* means a person with sufficient theoretical knowledge and practical experience to make an informed assessment of the likelihood of a dangerous atmosphere being present or subsequently arising in the space.

2.3 *Responsible person* means a person authorized to permit entry into an enclosed space and having sufficient knowledge of the procedures to be followed.

3 Assessment of risk

3.1 In order to ensure safety, a competent person should always make a preliminary assessment of any potential hazards in the space to be entered, taking into account previous cargo carried, ventilation of the space, coating of the space and other relevant factors. The competent person's preliminary assessment should determine the potential for the presence of an oxygen-deficient, flammable or toxic atmosphere.

3.2 The procedures to be followed for testing the atmosphere in the space and for entry should be decided on the basis of the preliminary assessment. These will depend on whether the preliminary assessment shows that:

.1 there is minimal risk to the health or life of personnel entering the space;

.2 there is no immediate risk to health or life but a risk could arise during the course of work in the space; and

.3 a risk to health or life is identified.

3.3   Where the preliminary assessment indicates minimal risk to health or life or potential for a risk to arise during the course of work in the space, the precautions described in 4, 5, 6 and 7 should be followed as appropriate.

3.4   Where the preliminary assessment identifies risk to life or health, if entry is to be made, the additional precautions specified in section 8 should also be followed.

4   Authorization of entry

4.1   No person should open or enter an enclosed space unless authorized by the master or nominated responsible person and unless the appropriate safety procedures laid down for the particular ship have been followed.

4.2   Entry into enclosed spaces should be planned and the use of an entry permit system, which may include the use of a checklist, is recommended. An Enclosed Space Entry Permit should be issued by the master or nominated responsible person, and completed by a person who enters the space prior to entry. An example of the Enclosed Space Entry Permit is provided in the appendix.

5   General precautions

5.1   The master or responsible person should determine that it is safe to enter an enclosed space by ensuring:

.1   that potential hazards have been identified in the assessment and as far as possible isolated or made safe;

.2   that the space has been thoroughly ventilated by natural or mechanical means to remove any toxic or flammable gases, and to ensure an adequate level of oxygen throughout the space;

.3   that the atmosphere of the space has been tested as appropriate with properly calibrated instruments to ascertain acceptable levels of oxygen and acceptable levels of flammable or toxic vapours;

.4   that the space has been secured for entry and properly illuminated;

.5   that a suitable system of communication between all parties for use during entry has been agreed and tested;

.6   that an attendant has been instructed to remain at the entrance to the space whilst it is occupied;

.7   that rescue and resuscitation equipment has been positioned ready for use at the entrance to the space, and that rescue arrangements have been agreed;

.8 that personnel are properly clothed and equipped for the entry and subsequent tasks; and

.9 that a permit has been issued authorizing entry.

The precautions in .6 and .7 may not apply to every situation described in this section. The person authorizing entry should determine whether an attendant and the positioning of rescue equipment at the entrance to the space is necessary.

5.2 Only trained personnel should be assigned the duties of entering, functioning as attendants, or functioning as members of rescue teams. Ships' crews should be drilled periodically in rescue and first aid.

5.3 All equipment used in connection with entry should be in good working condition and inspected prior to use.

6 Testing the atmosphere

6.1 Appropriate testing of the atmosphere of a space should be carried out with properly calibrated equipment by persons trained in the use of the equipment. The manufacturers' instructions should be strictly followed. Testing should be carried out before any person enters the space, and at regular intervals thereafter until all work is completed. Where appropriate, the testing of the space should be carried out at as many different levels as is necessary to obtain a representative sample of the atmosphere in the space.

6.2 For entry purposes, steady readings of the following should be obtained:

.1 21% oxygen by volume by oxygen content meter; and

.2 not more than 1% of lower flammable limit (LFL) on a suitably sensitive combustible-gas indicator, where the preliminary assessment has determined that there is potential for flammable gases or vapours.

If these conditions cannot be met, additional ventilation should be applied to the space and re-testing should be conducted after a suitable interval. Any gas testing should be carried out with ventilation to the enclosed space stopped, in order to obtain accurate readings.

6.3 Where the preliminary assessment has determined that there is potential for the presence of toxic gases and vapours, appropriate testing should be carried out using fixed or portable gas- or vapour-detection equipment. The readings obtained by this equipment should be below the occupational exposure limits for the toxic gases or vapours given in accepted national or international standards. It should be noted that testing for flammability does not provide a suitable means of measuring for toxicity, nor vice versa.

6.4   It should be emphasized that pockets of gas or oxygen-deficient areas can exist, and should always be suspected, even when an enclosed space has been satisfactorily tested as being suitable for entry.

7   Precautions during entry

7.1   The atmosphere should be tested frequently whilst the space is occupied, and persons should be instructed to leave the space should there be a deterioration in the conditions.

7.2   Ventilation should continue during the period that the space is occupied and during temporary breaks. Before re-entry after a break, the atmosphere should be re-tested. In the event of failure of the ventilation system, any persons in the space should leave immediately.

7.3   In the event of an emergency, under no circumstances should the attending crew member enter the space before help has arrived and the situation has been evaluated to ensure the safety of those entering the space to undertake rescue operations.

8   Additional precautions for entry into a space where the atmosphere is known or suspected to be unsafe

8.1   If the atmosphere in an enclosed space is suspected or known to be unsafe, the space should only be entered when no practical alternative exists. Entry should only be made for further testing, essential operation, safety of life or safety of a ship. The number of persons entering the space should be the minimum compatible with the work to be performed.

8.2   Suitable breathing apparatus, e.g., of the air-line or self-contained type, should always be worn, and only personnel trained in its use should be allowed to enter the space. Air-purifying respirators should not be used as they do not provide a supply of clean air from a source independent of the atmosphere within the space.

8.3   The precautions specified in 5 should also be followed, as appropriate.

8.4   Rescue harnesses should be worn and, unless impractical, lifelines should be used.

8.5   Appropriate protective clothing should be worn, particularly where there is any risk of toxic substances or chemicals coming into contact with the skin or eyes of those entering the space.

8.6 The advice in 7.3 concerning emergency rescue operations is particularly relevant in this context.

9 Hazards related to specific types of cargo

9.1 Dangerous goods in packaged form

9.1.1 The atmosphere of any space containing dangerous goods may put at risk the health or life of any person entering it. Dangers may include flammable, toxic or corrosive gases or vapours that displace oxygen, residues on packages and spilled material. The same hazards may be present in spaces adjacent to the cargo spaces. Information on the hazards of specific substances is contained in the IMDG Code, the Emergency Procedures for Ships Carrying Dangerous Goods (EmS)* and Materials Safety Data Sheets (MSDS). If there is evidence or suspicion that leakage of dangerous substances has occurred, the precautions specified in 8 should be followed.

9.1.2 Personnel required to deal with spillages or to remove defective or damaged packages should be appropriately trained and wear suitable breathing apparatus and appropriate protective clothing.

9.2 Bulk liquid

The tanker industry has produced extensive advice to operators and crews of ships engaged in the bulk carriage of oil, chemicals and liquefied gases, in the form of specialist international safety guides. Information in the guides on enclosed space entry amplifies these recommendations and should be used as the basis for preparing entry plans.

9.3 Solid bulk

On ships carrying solid bulk cargoes, dangerous atmospheres may develop in cargo spaces and adjacent spaces. The dangers may include flammability, toxicity, oxygen depletion or self-heating, which should be identified in shipping documentation. For additional information, reference should be made to the Code of Safe Practice for Solid Bulk Cargoes.

9.4 Oxygen-depleting cargoes and materials

A prominent risk with such cargoes is oxygen depletion due to the inherent form of the cargo, for example, self-heating, oxidation of metals and ores or decomposition of vegetable oils, animal fats, grain and other organic

---

* This has been superseded by *EmS Guide: Emergency Response Procedures for Ships Carrying Dangerous Goods* (see MSC/Circ.1025), which is associated with the IMDG Code as adopted by resolution MSC.122(75).

materials or their residues. The materials listed below are known to be capable of causing oxygen depletion. However, the list is not exhaustive. Oxygen depletion may also be caused by other materials of vegetable or animal origin, by flammable or spontaneously combustible materials, and by materials with a high metal content:

.1 grain, grain products and residues from grain processing (such as bran, crushed grain, crushed malt or meal), hops, malt husks and spent malt;

.2 oilseeds as well as products and residues from oilseeds (such as seed expellers, seed cake, oil cake and meal);

.3 copra;

.4 wood in such forms as packaged timber, roundwood, logs, pulpwood, props (pit props and other propwood), woodchips, woodshavings, woodpulp pellets and sawdust;

.5 jute, hemp, flax, sisal, kapok, cotton and other vegetable fibres (such as esparto grass/Spanish grass, hay, straw, bhusa), empty bags, cotton waste, animal fibres, animal and vegetable fabric, wool waste and rags;

.6 fishmeal and fishscrap;

.7 guano;

.8 sulphidic ores and ore concentrates;

.9 charcoal, coal and coal products;

.10 direct reduced iron (DRI)

.11 dry ice;

.12 metal wastes and chips, iron swarf, steel and other turnings, borings, drillings, shavings, filings and cuttings; and

.13 scrap metal.

9.5 Fumigation

When a ship is fumigated, the detailed recommendations contained in the Recommendations on the safe use of pesticides in ships[*] should be followed. Spaces adjacent to fumigated spaces should be treated as if fumigated.

---

[*] Refer to the Recommendations on safe use of pesticides in ships, approved by the Maritime Safety Committee of the Organization by circular MSC/Circ.612, as amended by MSC/Circ.689 and MSC/Circ.746.

10   Conclusion

Failure to observe simple procedures can lead to people being unexpectedly overcome when entering enclosed spaces. Observance of the principles outlined above will form a reliable basis for assessing risks in such spaces and for taking necessary precautions.

Appendix

Example of an Enclosed Space Entry Permit

This permit relates to entry into any enclosed space and should be completed by the master or responsible officer and by the person entering the space or authorized team leader.

General
Location/name of enclosed space
Reason for entry
This permit is valid from: . . . . hrs   Date . . . .
to: . . . . hrs   Date . . . .
(See note 1)

Section 1 – Pre-entry preparation		
(To be checked by the master or nominated responsible person)	Yes	No
Has the space been thoroughly ventilated?	☐	☐
Has the space been segregated by blanking off or isolating all connecting pipelines or valves and electrical power/equipment?	☐	☐
Has the space been cleaned where necessary?	☐	☐
Has the space been tested and found safe for entry? (See note 2)	☐	☐

Section 1 *(cont'd)*	Yes	No
Pre-entry atmosphere test readings:		
– oxygen . . . . % vol (21%)	By:	
– hydrocarbon . . . . % LFL (less than 1%)		
– toxic gases . . . . ppm (specific gas and PEL) (See note 3)	Time:	
Have arrangements been made for frequent atmosphere checks to be made while the space is occupied and after work breaks?	☐	☐
Have arrangements been made for the space to be continuously ventilated throughout the period of occupation and during work breaks?	☐	☐
Are access and illumination adequate?	☐	☐
Is rescue and resuscitation equipment available for immediate use by the entrance to the space?	☐	☐
Has a responsible person been designated to be in constant attendance at the entrance to the space?	☐	☐
Has the officer of the watch (bridge, engine-room, cargo control room) been advised of the planned entry?	☐	☐
Has a system of communication between all parties been tested and emergency signals agreed?	☐	☐
Are emergency and evacuation procedures established and understood by all personnel involved with the enclosed space entry?	☐	☐
Is all equipment used in good working condition and inspected prior to entry?	☐	☐
Are personnel properly clothed and equipped?	☐	☐

Section 2 – Pre-entry checks		
(To be checked by the person entering the space or authorized team leader)	Yes	No
I have received instructions or permission from the master or nominated responsible person to enter the enclosed space	☐	☐
Section 1 of this permit has been satisfactorily completed by the master or nominated responsible person	☐	☐
I have agreed and understand the communication procedures	☐	☐
I have agreed upon a reporting interval of . . . . minutes	☐	☐

Section 2 *(cont'd)*	Yes	No
Emergency and evacuation procedures have been agreed and are understood	☐	☐
I am aware that the space must be vacated immediately in the event of ventilation failure or if atmosphere tests show a change from agreed safe criteria	☐	☐

Section 3 – Breathing apparatus and other equipment		
(To be checked jointly by the master or nominated responsible person and the person who is to enter the space)	Yes	No
Those entering the space are familiar with the breathing apparatus to be used	☐	☐
The breathing apparatus has been tested as follows:		
– gauge and capacity of air supply	. . . .	
– low pressure audible alarm	. . . .	
– face mask – under positive pressure and not leaking	. . . .	
The means of communication has been tested and emergency signals agreed	☐	☐
All personnel entering the space have been provided with rescue harnesses and, where practicable, lifelines	☐	☐

Signed upon completion of sections 1, 2 and 3 by:

Master or nominated responsible person . . . .

Date . . . . Time . . . .

Responsible person supervising entry . . . .

Date . . . . Time . . . .

Person entering the space or authorized team leader

Date . . . . Time . . . .

Section 4 – Personnel entry

(To be completed by the responsible person
supervising entry)

Names	Time in	Time out
. . . .	. . . .	. . . .
. . . .	. . . .	. . . .
. . . .	. . . .	. . . .
. . . .	. . . .	. . . .

Section 5 – Completion of job

(To be completed by the responsible person
supervising entry)

Job completed   Date . . . . Time . . . .

Space secured against entry   Date . . . . Time . . . .

The officer of the watch has been duly informed Date . . . . Time . . . .

Signed upon completion of sections 4 and 5 by:

Responsible person supervising entry . . . .

Date . . . . Time . . . .

THIS PERMIT IS RENDERED INVALID SHOULD VENTILATION OF THE SPACE
STOP OR IF ANY OF THE CONDITIONS NOTED IN THE CHECKLIST CHANGE

Notes:

1 The permit should contain a clear indication as to its maximum period of validity.

2 In order to obtain a representative cross-section of the space's atmosphere, samples should be taken from several levels and through as many openings as possible. Ventilation should be stopped for about 10 min before the pre-entry atmosphere tests are taken.

3 Tests for specific toxic contaminants, such as benzene or hydrogen sulphide, should be undertaken depending on the nature of the previous contents of the space.

Enclosed spaces can kill!

Do not ignore or forget it –

you may end up like this ...